WHAT OTHERS ARE SAYING A

"This is an outstanding book, absolutely ~~~~ ~
every entrepreneur. Every page contains practical ideas that can save you thousands of dollars and hundreds of hours in starting or building your business."
—BRIAN TRACY, *Chairman, Brian Tracy International*
Sales and management consultant and trainer

"A wicked good, practical, tactical guide for making your American dream a reality."
—DOUG HALL, *CEO, Eureka! Ranch*
Marketing maverick; Author of Jump Start Your Brain

"*Business Start-up Guide* is a practical book for beginning entrepreneurs that offers step-by-step guidance and advice to help you get started. Preparation is a key ingredient to properly starting and operating a small business. Tom Severance's Guide will help you prepare your business plan and understand what it takes to be successful."
—HAL LEFKOWITZ, *Director, Small Business Development Center of the Greater San Diego Chamber of Commerce*

"*Business Start-up Guide* is a comprehensive guide every start-up business person should read. It walks you through all the basics and much more."
—PAMELA WILLIS, *Executive Director, San Diego Business Innovation Center*

"This Guide is an excellent compilation of the essential challenges and solutions for any new business. Tom Severance brings a unique perspective to the Guide—as a business expert, a certified public accountant, and an attorney. I recommend it to anyone considering a new business or needing to solve problems in an existing company."
—JAMES A. BOYCE, *President, Rancho Santa Fe National Bank*

BUSINESS START-UP GUIDE

How to Create, Grow, and Manage Your Own Successful Enterprise

Tom Severance

Tycoon Publishing
Oceanside, California

Business Start-up Guide
How to Create, Grow, and Manage Your Own Successful Enterprise

by Tom Severance

edited by Becky Colgan
designed by Sci-Tech Communications

Published by Tycoon Publishing
3809 Plaza Drive, #107-111
Oceanside, CA 92056

This book is designed to provide general information on starting and running a business. It is sold with the understanding that the publisher and author are not engaged in rendering specific legal, tax, accounting, or other professional advice or services. If legal or other expert assistance is required, seek the services of a competent professional.

The purpose of this guide is to educate and entertain. It is designed to complement, amplify, and supplement other texts. You are encouraged to read all the available material, learn as much as possible about entrepreneurship, and to tailor the information to your individual needs.

Every effort has been made to make this book as complete and as accurate as possible. However, there may be mistakes both typographical and in content. Therefore, this text should be used only as a general guide and not as the ultimate source of business information. Furthermore, this book contains information on business only up to the printing date.

Publisher's Cataloging-in-Publication
(Provided by Quality Books, Inc.)

Severance, Tom.
      Business start-up guide : how to create, grow, and manage your own successful enterprise / Tom Severance ; [edited by Becky Colgan].
      p. cm.
      Includes bibliographical references and index.
      LCCN: 97-90802
      ISBN 0-9653212-0-7

  1. New business enterprises—Management. 2. Entrepreneurship.
3. Success in business. I. Colgan, Becky, ed. II. Title.

HD62.5.S48 1998   658.4'21
                 QBI97-1530

Table of Contents

About the Author

Tom Severance is an Attorney at Law and Certified Public Accountant. His practice, Severance & Associates, Inc., based in San Diego, California, specializes in business, real estate, tax, and estate planning issues. Tom has prior legal, accounting, and tax experience with Coopers & Lybrand and the Internal Revenue Service.

Tom is also a full-time business instructor at MiraCosta College in Oceanside, California. He is in charge of all management, marketing, law, tax, entrepreneur, and international business courses. Tom is also Director of the Entrepreneur Center at the school. The Entrepreneur Center provides students and the business community with access to business books, periodicals, audiotapes, videotapes, and computer software.

Tom is a frequent speaker in the business community. He has taught classes and presented seminars on entrepreneurship, marketing, finance, accounting, law, and tax to many groups over the years, including

Becker CPA Review	San Diego Career Centers
California Western School of Law	San Diego SBDC
Grossmont College	SBA-SCORE
National University	Southwestern College
San Diego Community College	UCSD Extension

Tom is originally from Rochester, Minnesota. He received his Bachelor of Science degree in Business Administration from Arizona State University, in Tempe, Arizona, and his JD and MBA degrees from the University of Minnesota, in Minneapolis, Minnesota.

Severance & Associates, Inc.   Phone: (619) 481-1171
12925 El Camino Real, Suite J23   Fax: (619) 481-6519
San Diego, CA 92130-1893   Fax-on-Demand: (619) 755-3118
E-mail: tseveran@severance.com
Internet: http://www.severance.com

Preface

Congratulations! Starting and running your own business can be the culmination of the American dream. Success requires careful planning and execution. Applying the principles in this book is a great start.

This book is the result of a sabbatical leave project at MiraCosta College in Oceanside, California. It synthesizes the best information and ideas from my teaching, counseling, and business ownership experience. It also blends the best ideas from the substantial business literature that I reviewed and studied during my sabbatical.

Read, review, and ponder the information and ideas in this book. Apply the practical exercises at the end of each chapter to really learn and drive home the points.

Please inform me of your successes and suggestions. I hope this book will serve as a valuable tool.

Acknowledgments

This book is dedicated to my parents, Lewis and Rachel Severance, for their love and support over the years.

Thank you to the people who reviewed and made suggestions for improvement of the book in substance, procedure, and design:

Gary Apger	Erik Lund
Malcolm Avner	Mike Malchiodi
Leon Baradat	Jill Malone
David Branfman	Tom Morrow
Craig Castanos	Val Myers
Bill Eigner	Dave Nydegger
Barbara Eldridge	Linda Osborne
Marion Foerster	Sandi Peterson
Michael Gerber	Dan Poynter
Phil Gilbert	Linda Ramsay
Alleen Gleason	Chris Reardon
Art Goodman	Sheila Robbins
Rose Gow	Gary Severance
Leslynn Grandy	Paul Severance
Marilyn Grant	Lee Silber
Bob Hickethier	Jim Stanton
Jan Krieg	Andy Townsend
Lynda Lee	Craig Ulbrich
Hal Lefkowitz	Mike Wilson

Thank you to the full-time faculty members of the MiraCosta College Business Department for their support over the years:

Paul Basart	Jim Stanton
Bob Edmondson	Sue Stacy
Jill Malone	Andy Townsend

Thank you to the members of the MiraCosta College Board of Trustees for their support and approval of my sabbatical project:

Carolyn Batiste	Henry Holloway
Diane Bessell	Robert Kleffel
Gloria Carranza	Jean Moreno
Tim Dong	Carol Smith

CHAPTER 1

Are You an Entrepreneur?

Money, security, confidence, peace of mind, and a strong sense of accomplishment are all yours as you relax on the beach and enjoy the tropical wonders of the Bahamas. Of course, you worked very hard to start and grow your business. You followed a well-thought-out business plan. It wasn't easy, but no one said it would or should be. You can now enjoy a well-deserved vacation, knowing the business is still making money for you back home. You're here to relax and enjoy the fruits of your labor with your family. Who knows? You might even come up with some creative new business ideas to implement when you return home. Just let your mind take you where it wants.

Is this fiction or reality? You could be in this position within a few years if you really want to start and grow a business, and if you plan properly and work hard. You certainly may be able to improve your financial status. Nevertheless, remember it's the intangibles that make running your own business such a joy.

This chapter will help you make the important decision of whether you should start your own business. You've probably made your mind up already, but go through the analysis suggested here anyway. It will help you make or confirm a well-reasoned, rational, unemotional decision.

WHY START A BUSINESS?

People start businesses for many different reasons. The two most common are

⟶ To be independent, to be their own boss, and to have more control over their destiny

⟶ To have unlimited earning potential

Additional reasons include

- To gain recognition and respect from others
- To be able to use their creativity
- To build a family business with their name
- To turn a hobby into a paying business
- To be able to work until they want to retire
- To take a risk on their abilities and interests
- To do something they enjoy
- To grow and develop skills and abilities
- To work on the days and hours they desire
- To supplement the family income
- To avoid being laid off or terminated by an employer

You might question the wisdom or truth of some of these reasons. The above list may or may not reflect your own motivations. However, recognize that the reasons listed above reflect only the positive side of starting a business. There are also many reasons why 80 percent of the working population don't start a business. Whatever your motivating factors are, be sure to match your desires with a successful business idea using the steps discussed in chapter 2.

Even if you have been content working for others as an employee, you may soon need to become an entrepreneur. You may be marketing a product you've developed or marketing your own services as a self-employed person because of down-sizing, right-sizing, restructuring, reductions in force, or cutbacks.

William Bridges, author of *JobShift,* claims that the "late, great job" is rapidly disappearing. The old rules are gone. The new rules, according to Bridges, are

- Everyone is a contingent worker with their continued employment contingent on the results they produce.

- Workers need to demonstrate their value to the organization in each successive situation.
- Workers need to see themselves as "in business for themselves" with their tasks outsourced to them by the organization.
- Workers need to take primary responsibility for their career-long self-development, compensation, and benefits.
- Workers must be able to work in project teams and be able to shift their focus rapidly from one task to another.
- Workers must be able to work without clear job descriptions and to work on several projects at once.
- Long-term employment is a thing of the past for most workers.

To see the advantages and disadvantages more clearly, use the Ben Franklin method for making a rational decision. Take out a clean piece of paper and draw a vertical line down the middle. On the left side, write "Advantages" at the top. On the right side, write "Disadvantages" at the top. Seriously think and reflect on the benefits and concerns that relate specifically to you. This is a great exercise for group brainstorming. You will discover benefits and concerns you didn't think of on your own.

Subdivide each section into "Personal and Family," "Financial and Tax," and "Career and Social." In each of these categories list advantages and disadvantages of starting and running a business. After listing all you can by yourself or with the help of others, how does the analysis look? Have you listed more advantages or more disadvantages? Which are the most important to you? What is the most logical decision to make? If you plan to go ahead with a business, can you eliminate or minimize some of the disadvantages? To help you get started, take a look at some typical responses for each of the six categories on page 14.

Be realistic in your expectations. You will very likely work harder and longer hours in your own business. You will likely earn less money in the short term than you would working for someone else. Make sure the intangible benefits and the long-term financial outlook override these probabilities.

TYPICAL ADVANTAGES AND DISADVANTAGES

ADVANTAGES	DISADVANTAGES
Personal and Family	
1. Being my own boss	1. Loss of recreational and family time
2.	2.
3.	3.
4.	4.
5.	5.
Financial and Tax	
1. Unlimited earning potential	1. Loss of corporate fringe benefits
2.	2.
3.	3.
4.	4.
5.	5.
Career and Social	
1. Ability to use and develop new skills	1. Less people contact (with few or no employees)
2.	2.
3.	3.
4.	4.
5.	5.

ENTREPRENEUR MYTHS AND TRAITS

There are many misconceptions about who entrepreneurs are and how they function. Jeffrey Timmons, author of *New Venture Creation*, cites the following fifteen myths and the reality behind them:

Myth 1: Entrepreneurs are born, not made.
Reality: While entrepreneurs are born with certain native intelligence, a flair for creativity, and energy, these talents by themselves are like unmolded clay or an unpainted canvas. The making of an entrepreneur occurs by accumulating the relevant skills, knowledge, experiences, and contacts over a period of years. It includes large doses of self-development. The creative capacity to envision and pursue an opportunity is a direct descendant of at least ten or more years of experience.

Myth 2: Anyone can start a business.
Reality: Entrepreneurs who recognize the difference between an idea and an opportunity, and who can visualize potential, start

businesses that have a better chance of succeeding. Luck, if involved, requires good preparation. Starting the business is often the easiest part. Surviving, sustaining, and building a venture so that its founders can realize the reward is often the hardest part. Perhaps only 5 percent to 10 percent of all new businesses that survive five or more years produce an eventual capital gain for the founders.

Myth 3: Entrepreneurs are gamblers.
Reality: Successful entrepreneurs take carefully calculated risks. They try to influence the odds, often by getting others to share risk with them and by avoiding or minimizing risks. They often slice the risk into smaller, quite digestible pieces. Only then do they commit the time or resources to determine if that piece will work. They do not deliberately seek to take more risk or unnecessary risk. However, they do not shy away from unavoidable risk.

Myth 4: Entrepreneurs want the whole show to themselves.
Reality: Owning and running the whole show effectively puts a ceiling on growth. Solo entrepreneurs usually make a living. It is extremely difficult to grow a higher potential venture by working single-handedly. Higher potential entrepreneurs build a team, an organization, and a company. Remember that 100 percent of nothing is nothing. Rather than taking a large piece of the pie, work to make the pie bigger.

Myth 5: Entrepreneurs are their own bosses and completely independent.
Reality: Entrepreneurs are far from independent. They have to serve many masters and constituencies, including partners, investors, customers, suppliers, creditors, employees, families, and those involved in social and community obligations. Entrepreneurs, however, can make free choices of whether and when they care to respond. Moreover, it is difficult and rare to single-handedly build a business beyond $1 million to $2 million in sales.

Myth 6: Entrepreneurs work longer and harder than managers in big companies.
Reality: There is no evidence that all entrepreneurs work more than their corporate counterparts. Some do and some do not. Working long days and working on weekends are typical for all successful business people.

Myth 7: Entrepreneurs experience a great deal of stress and pay a high price.

Reality: Being an entrepreneur is stressful and demanding. However, there is no evidence that it is any more stressful than numerous other highly demanding professional roles. Entrepreneurs find their jobs very satisfying. They have a high sense of accomplishment, are healthier, and are much less likely to want to retire than those who work for others. Three times as many entrepreneurs as corporate managers say they never plan to retire because they enjoy their work so much.

Myth 8: Starting a business is risky and often ends in failure.

Reality: Talented and experienced entrepreneurs pursue attractive opportunities and attract the right people and the necessary financial and other resources to make the venture work. Businesses fail, but true entrepreneurs do not. Failure is often the fire that tempers the steel of an entrepreneur's learning experience and street savvy.

Myth 9: Money is the most important start-up ingredient.

Reality: If the other pieces and talents are there, the money will follow. However, it does not follow that an entrepreneur will succeed if he or she has enough money. Money will definitely not guarantee success. Nevertheless, ensure you have sufficient funds or access to funds to survive the start-up phase. Chapter 13 discusses this issue. Money is to the entrepreneur what the paint and brush are to the artist—an inert tool that, in the right hands, can create marvels. Money is also a way of keeping score, rather than just an end in itself. Entrepreneurs thrive on the thrill of the chase. Even after a true entrepreneur has made substantial money, he or she will often work incessantly on a new vision to build another company.

Myth 10: Entrepreneurs should be young and energetic.

Reality: While these qualities may help, age is no barrier. The average age of entrepreneurs starting high-potential businesses is in the mid-thirties. There are also many examples of entrepreneurs starting businesses in their sixties. What is critical is possessing the relevant knowledge, experience, and contacts that greatly facilitate recognizing and pursuing an opportunity.

Myth 11: The quest for the almighty dollar is the sole motivation for entrepreneurs.

Reality: Entrepreneurs seeking high-potential ventures are driven more by building enterprises and realizing long-term capital gains than by instant gratification through high salaries and perks. A sense of personal achievement and accomplishment, feeling in control of their own destiny, and realizing their vision and dreams are other powerful motivators. Entrepreneurs view money as a tool and a way of keeping score.

Myth 12: Entrepreneurs seek power and control over others.

Reality: The quest for responsibility and achievement, rather than power for its own sake, drives successful entrepreneurs. They thrive on a sense of accomplishment and outperforming the competition, rather than a personal need for power expressed by dominating and controlling others. By virtue of their accomplishments, they may be powerful and influential, but these are more the by-products of the entrepreneurial process than a driving force behind it.

Myth 13: If an entrepreneur is talented, success will happen in one or two years.

Reality: An old maxim among venture capitalists says it all: The lemons ripen in two or three years, but the pearls take seven or eight. A new business rarely establishes itself in less than three or four years.

Myth 14: Any entrepreneur with a good idea can raise venture capital.

Reality: Venture capitalists fund only 1 percent to 3 percent of the ideas submitted to them.

Myth 15: If an entrepreneur has enough start-up capital, he or she can't miss.

Reality: The opposite is often true. Too much money at the outset often creates euphoria and a spoiled-child syndrome. The accompanying lack of discipline and impulsive spending habits often lead to serious problems and failure.

There are a variety of tests that help assess your potential entrepreneurial success. Most calculate a numerical score that you can then compare with what "typical" or "successful" entrepreneurs score. These are fun and entertaining, especially if you score well.

The answers that tend to indicate entrepreneurial ability are usually quite obvious, so it is important to answer the questions without trying to guess the preferred response. Of course, the test merely compares your results with what the author believes are the best entrepreneurial responses. It is not scientific, and there are certainly many exceptions to the standard. Take the tests. They're interesting, and you may learn something, but don't take the results too seriously.

Common sense and experience should persuade you that successful entrepreneurs have certain traits. You would likely describe the prototype *perfect entrepreneur* as follows:

- A goal setter who writes down clear, realistic, challenging, attainable objectives
- Tenacious, determined, and patient enough to complete the job
- Honest, fair, optimistic, cooperative, and tactful
- A straightforward and effective verbal and written communicator
- Self-confident and self-directed
- Driven to compete and succeed against self-imposed standards
- Not afraid of failure; able to deal with and learn from it
- A moderate risk-taker who takes carefully calculated risks with a strong chance for success
- A decision-maker who takes the initiative
- A hands-on learner
- Has a strong drive and energy level maintained through good diet and exercise habits
- A *smart* worker as well as a *hard* worker
- Open-minded with a tolerance for ambiguity and uncertainty
- Exercises practical judgment with good critical thinking skills, problem-solving ability, and creativity
- Aware of personal strengths and weaknesses and the appropriate use of outside resource people
- Has specialized technical knowledge within the business

- Has good numbers sense and strong analytical ability
- Has a healthy respect for money and the ability to use it effectively and appropriately

SUGGESTIONS FOR SUCCESS

The E Myth: Why Most Small Businesses Don't Work and What To Do About It, by Michael E. Gerber, brings a unique perspective to entrepreneurship. The myth is that a "technician," who is skilled in performing everyday tasks in the business, will succeed in running that same business.

Gerber points out that many people go into business only when stricken with an "entrepreneurial seizure." This often occurs just after getting into an argument with the boss or after working on a weekend project without appropriate rewards and enjoyment. Suddenly, these employees, who perform the technical work of the job very well, decide they can do even better starting and running their own business. This is very dangerous thinking. The fatal assumption of many prospective entrepreneurs is that "if you understand the technical work of a business, you understand a business that does the technical work." These are two totally different skills that many do not realize until it's too late.

The three skills of *technician*, *manager*, and *entrepreneur* are in everyone, but to different degrees. The technician is the doer who lives in the present. The manager is the pragmatic problem-solver who craves order and lives in the past. The entrepreneur is the visionary and dreamer who lives in the future. Ideally, one starting a business would have a good balance of each. However, experience indicates that the typical small business owner is more likely to be 10 percent entrepreneur, 20 percent manager, and 70 percent technician.

Develop and run your business as a *franchise prototype.* Treat your business as if you will eventually franchise it, even if you have no such intentions. This mind-set allows you to develop a turnkey operation that will eventually run by itself. Work *on* your business, not *in* it.

Systematically set and apply appropriate strategy to all the decisions in your business. Continue learning and improving in all aspects of the business through *innovation, quantification,* and *orchestration.* Think of potential new ideas or approaches in all parts of your business, determine ways to test the ideas, and, if they work, implement them. Continue until you find a better, more effective way. Always be on the lookout for improvements and for better, more effective methods.

Entrepreneurs often overlook three other important items. You need to confront several issues if you are leaving an employment position. You must discuss long-term business goals with any other owners or major participants. You may also need to address the issues raised by business involvement of family members.

If you are leaving regular employment, here are some suggestions for what you should do before giving up the security of W-2 income:

- ✓ Check your employment contract for any competition restrictions.
- ✓ Consider health insurance continuation under applicable federal and state laws.
- ✓ Consider obtaining or increasing liability, disability, or term life insurance.
- ✓ Arrange for credit and loans before you discontinue the secure W-2 income that bankers love.
- ✓ Conserve cash by planning appropriately, postponing expenditures, and using credit judiciously.
- ✓ If you plan to operate out of your home, make sure you can legally operate with the necessary licenses.
- ✓ Open a separate business checking account and start keeping complete and accurate business records.
- ✓ Socialize and meet people by becoming active in professional organizations and other groups.

Long-term goals of individual business owners must be clear. For businesses with more than one owner, the goals of all owners should be clear and consistent with each other. Many believe that everyone who starts a business automatically wants to grow the business as large as possible, and to make as much money as possible. While this is certainly true of some, it is by no means true of all. It is probably not true of most entrepreneurs.

It is helpful to classify new businesses as one of three types: lifestyle, mid-size, or high-growth. Each has its advantages and disadvantages. The important point is to realize which type you are and want to be. Ensure that all owners understand and agree.

The two major factors that determine the classification are the projected sales and the projected number of employees. You often must use and leverage money and people to grow a business. The proper use and management of money and people can be the biggest advantage in growing a business. The improper use and management of money and people can be the biggest disaster.

A **lifestyle** business is the most common type started, although not always intentionally. Entrepreneurs who want to maximize independence, autonomy, and control often start lifestyle businesses. Neither large sales nor large profits are important, beyond providing a sufficient and comfortable living. Lifestyle entrepreneurs don't want the headaches that come with growth and the need for more employees and capital. They need minimal outside financing and utilize few employees. A self-employed business consultant working out of the home is a good example of a lifestyle business.

A **mid-size** business usually employs larger assets and more employees to earn higher profits. Profit is more important than sales. The owner relinquishes some autonomy and control. The owner needs to deal with banks and employment issues but is still able to maintain 100 percent ownership. There is rarely a need for outside investors or venture capitalists. The local fast food restaurant is a good example of a mid-size business.

A **high-growth** business shoots for the stars. Initially, sales are more important than profits. Later, profits also become important. The goal is to build a nationally or internationally known enterprise. There will be problems and opportunities with banks and employees. Investors and venture capitalists may insist on taking over ownership and control. Apple Computer and Microsoft are good examples of high-growth businesses.

Give some thought to your goals and objectives in starting, running, and growing a business. Realize that these three classifications are a continuum and not exact positions. Knowing what you and others want, and realizing the advantages and disadvantages, is very important.

Family businesses can be a source of great joy and togetherness. They can also be the source of numerous conflicts. Understand that families and businesses have different purposes, goals, and values. The participants also play different roles in each.

The family system is emotion-based, with caring and sharing, and there is a lifetime membership. The business system is unemotional, task-based, with performance rewarded. There is a "perform or leave" approach. It is impossible to prevent all overlap of family and business systems. Nevertheless, try to minimize the overlap. Too much overlap can cause conflict when the systems have such radically different goals and values.

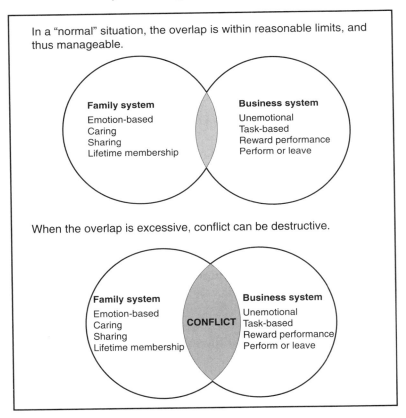

In a "normal" situation, the overlap is within reasonable limits, and thus manageable.

Family system
Emotion-based
Caring
Sharing
Lifetime membership

Business system
Unemotional
Task-based
Reward performance
Perform or leave

When the overlap is excessive, conflict can be destructive.

Family system
Emotion-based
Caring
Sharing
Lifetime membership

CONFLICT

Business system
Unemotional
Task-based
Reward performance
Perform or leave

Arthur Pine, author of *Your Family Business*, lists these basic principles for family harmony on the job:

- Really love the business. Truly enjoy it.
- Really love being together. Connect well at home before you consider working together in the office.

- If your dream is to bring family into the business, tell them. Talk openly about the possibilities.
- Be sure there is a mutual willingness to work together. If the ability is there, let the younger generation make the final decision.
- Take the view that working together is an opportunity, not an obligation.
- Pinpoint your motives for working together, and confirm that they are beneficial for the business and yourself.
- Treat each other as valued partners in the business.
- Respect all the years of success and hard work that went into the family business before you became a part of it.
- Respect the good ideas each member of the family will generate in years to come.
- Give the space and freedom necessary for a new generation to find its own niche, its own style of doing business.
- Divide responsibilities fairly, according to talents.
- Treat family members as who they are, not whom you wish they would be.
- Do not take away responsibilities once you have delegated them.
- Actively listen to each other.
- Solicit opinions. Common sense knows no age and often provides the most obvious solutions.
- Keep politics out of the family business.
- Openly and mutually establish a trial basis for working together, with competence being the sole criterion.
- Distance personal emotions from business decisions. In the office, put the business first.
- Confront conflicts, work to resolve them, and then let them go.
- Avoid taking sides when others in the family fight. Try to let them work together to resolve their conflict.
- Show no favoritism among family members in the firm.

- Treat relatives as fair job candidates first and as family second.
- Give space to family members so that they can develop their personal lives.
- Pick your battles carefully.
- Keep and cultivate a sense of humor.
- Admit when you are wrong.
- Be flexible, open to change, and open to criticism.
- Welcome criticism and suggestions for improving work style.
- Communicate on everything. Keep each other up-to-date.
- Be open and willing to ask questions, and to answer them.
- Give honest compliments to each other. Seek out areas and actions to compliment.
- Champion each other's success in the business. Support each other.
- Determine that your mutual goals for the business are compatible.
- Do not expect perfection. There is no such thing.
- Do not set unrealistic goals for family members that you would not set for others.
- Treat family with the same respect and trust that you do other valued employees.
- Treat nonfamily employees as you would family.
- Keep your temper in check.
- Avoid blaming each other for making mistakes. Ask not what you did wrong, but what you can do to make it right.
- Don't try to change each other's work habits if the business is thriving.
- Don't search out each other's faults. Search for and acknowledge each other's strengths.
- Be open with trusted nonfamily members about the future and where they stand in the company.
- Keep your privileges, but let the younger generation know they too will earn them someday.
- Call on trusted nonfamily members to help resolve business debates and conflicts. Implement what is best for the business.

- Hold no grudges.
- Put more value on intelligence than on age.
- Plan together for the future well-being of the business when the family first becomes involved.
- Establish a financial plan for succession, and make it clear to everyone in the firm what the line of succession will be.

Post the official credo of the American Entrepreneurs Association on your bathroom mirror. Reading it enthusiastically is a great way to start your day. It will be especially motivating when times are toughest.

THE ENTREPRENEUR'S CREDO

I do not choose to be a common person.
It is my right to be uncommon—if I can.
I seek opportunity—not security.
I do not wish to be a kept citizen, humbled
and dulled by having the state look after me.

I want to take the calculated risk;
to dream and to build,
to fail and to succeed.

I refuse to barter incentive for a dole;
I prefer the challenges of life
to the guaranteed existence;
the thrill of fulfillment to the stale calm of Utopia.

I will not trade freedom for beneficence
nor my dignity for a handout.
I will never cower before any master
nor bend to any threat.

It is my heritage to stand erect,
proud and unafraid; to think and act for myself,
to enjoy the benefit of my creations
and to face the world boldly and say:
This, with God's help, I have done.
All this is what it means to be an entrepreneur.

CHAPTER 1
ACTION ITEMS

Are You an Entrepreneur?

1. Complete your own Advantages and Disadvantages List for starting your business.

2. Determine whether you plan to operate a lifestyle, mid-size, or high-growth business, and explain your rationale.

3. Explain your philosophy for having or not having family members involved in your business.

CHAPTER 2

Finding and Evaluating Business Ideas

Trailblazing into undiscovered territory with a new business is very exciting. However, think through your decision before jumping in head first. Don't let the excitement of this new beginning prevent careful planning and analysis. This chapter discusses the two distinct topics of finding and evaluating potential business ideas.

FINDING BUSINESS IDEAS

Three different types of students attend entrepreneurship classes. Some are ready to start a business very shortly, and they know exactly what they want to do. Others want to start soon, but they have no firm business idea in mind. Others are dreamers who have no ideas and no time frame.

There is an advantage to knowing what business you want to start, assuming it matches the criteria discussed in the next section. However, there is also an advantage to having an open mind in deciding what type of business to start. If you are open to ideas, you can let the market decide for you, at least initially. It's much easier to find a need and fill it than to insist on selling a certain product or service and hoping the market will buy it.

Even if you have a general idea of the type of business you plan to start, be flexible as to your market niche. Not only is this wise when starting the business, but it is necessary as you grow the business. The pace of change in most areas today is so rapid that a successful entrepreneur needs to be flexible and receptive to such changes.

It's important to clearly distinguish the concepts of *finding an idea* and *evaluating an idea.* Finding possible ideas should be freewheeling, creative, and open-minded. Evaluating ideas requires a more structured and practical approach.

Brainstorming is a very effective way to generate ideas. Evaluation comes later. The basic rules to effective brainstorming for you and your group are

- Forbid judgment and criticism.
- Welcome wild, crazy, off-the-wall, freewheeling ideas.
- Strive for *quantity* of ideas rather than quality of ideas.
- Combine, improve, and build on others' ideas.
- Make sure all participants understand the rules.
- Have a nonparticipant record every idea.

Keep your eyes, ears, and mind alert and open as you proceed through your daily routine. There are business possibilities everywhere. Instead of seeing problems and becoming upset when something doesn't work or when you can't find something, think of it as a business opportunity. There are likely many others who have the same need.

Here's a great list of ways to stimulate idea creation:

- Read your local and metropolitan newspapers.
- Read *USA Today.*
- Read the *Wall Street Journal* and *New York Times.*
- Read the popular consumer and news magazines.
- Join associations that serve the industry you're considering.
- Review the fiction and nonfiction best-seller lists.
- Visit the public library and browse.
- Review government and consumer publications.

- Subscribe to relevant trade periodicals and magazines.
- Attend industry conventions and trade shows.
- Go online and keep up with the latest information.
- Browse through the Yellow Pages of your phone book.
- Watch and review the top ten prime-time television shows.
- Pay attention to commercials.
- Visit a good business library and browse.
- Review *Standard Rate and Data Service* (*SRDS*).
- Review the *Thomas Register of American Manufacturers*.
- Review the *Encyclopedia of Associations*.
- Browse through the magazine section of a bookstore.
- Walk through your local mall with analytical eyes.
- Visit your local Small Business Association (SBA) office.
- Visit your local chamber of commerce.
- Analyze whether your hobbies are a potential business.
- Look for obvious needs and wants that aren't being satisfied.
- Read the latest *Occupational Outlook Handbook*, published by the U.S. Department of Labor.
- Check out the business opportunity ads in the classifieds.
- Visit a business broker.
- Visit a career counselor and take the interest and aptitude tests.
- Obtain a part-time job in an industry that interests you.
- Visit and talk with those in the industry you're considering.
- Attend interesting business seminars and workshops.
- Review your past experiences, interests, and successes.

Management guru Peter Drucker, author of *Innovation and Entrepreneurship*, discusses seven specific sources for innovative opportunity. Keep these sources in mind. They may trigger a great idea.

The first four sources lie within the enterprise and are visible primarily to people within that sector. These four highly reliable indicators of change are

- **The unexpected**—the unexpected success, the unexpected failure, the unexpected outside event
- **The incongruity** between reality as it actually is and reality as it is assumed to be or as it "ought to be"
- **Innovation based on process need**
- **Changes in industry structure or market structure** that catch everyone unaware

The three sources that involve changes outside the enterprise or industry are

⟶ **Demographics** (population changes)
⟶ **Changes in perception, mood, and meaning**
⟶ **Scientific and nonscientific new knowledge**

Use an idea-generating checklist to solve a problem or to spark new ideas and insights.

Specifically, when assessing a product or service, ask yourself the following questions:

- Can it be *put to other uses*? Are there other ways to use it as is? Are there other uses if modified?
- Can it be *adapted*? What else is like this? What other idea does this suggest? Does the past offer a parallel? What could I copy? Whom could I emulate?
- Can it be *modified*? New twist? New meaning, color, motion, sound, odor, form, shape?
- Can it be *magnified*? What to add? More time? Greater frequency? Stronger? Higher? Longer? Thicker? Extra value? Duplicate? Multiply? Exaggerate?
- Can it be *minimized*? What to subtract? Smaller? Condensed? Miniature? Lower? Shorter? Lighter? Omit? Streamline? Split up? Understate?

- Can something be *substituted?* Who? What? Other material, process? Other power, place, approach, tone of voice?
- Can it be *rearranged?* Interchange components? Other pattern, layout, sequence? Transpose cause and effect? Change pace, schedule?
- Can it be *reversed?* Transpose positive and negative? How about opposites? Turn it backward, upside down? Reverse roles? Change shoes? Turn tables?
- Can it be *combined?* Blend, alloy, assortment, ensemble? Combine units, purposes, appeals, ideas?

EVALUATING BUSINESS IDEAS

Ideas are a dime a dozen. People who put them into practice are priceless. You need to go beyond dreaming. Nevertheless, evaluate all business ideas carefully before taking action.

Your best chance for success depends on several factors. If you can honestly answer yes to the four following questions, you've probably found the business for you. Answering yes to three of four is still encouraging. However, if you answer yes to only one or two, the odds of success and happiness dwindle.

Question 1: Do you love the business?
Question 2: Are you skilled at the business?
Question 3: Do you have experience in the business?
Question 4: Is the business a trend?

As far as "loving" the business, would you still start and operate this business if there was no monetary compensation? Imagine you just won $10 million in the state lottery or you just inherited $10 million. You don't need to work another day in your life. Of course you take some time off to celebrate and enjoy your winnings. It might be a week, a month, a year, or more. Regardless, there comes a time when you want to do something productive. Would this be the business? If you can honestly answer yes, congratulations! You love the business.

Make sure you are skilled at what you do. You have unique abilities and talents to use in your life. Are those talents and abilities useful and appropriate to the business? Are you putting your skills and talents to their best use? Strive to be the best in your field and an acknowledged expert in the subject area.

Experience can come through working in a similar business or through education in your industry. Any work in the business, even if low-level or part-time, is very valuable. Learn as much as you can about the business and all employment positions. Always be thinking about what you could improve if and when you are in a business ownership position.

Carefully analyze each new business, new product, and new idea to determine whether it is *on trend, off trend, or neutral.* Trends change over time, and people differ in their assessment of trends, so use an updated trend list that is consistent with your opinions when doing this analysis. Run the business or idea through your personally developed list of major trends. Use a little imagination to determine if it is consistent with each of the trends. If it supports at least four trends, you're on the right track. More than four is a bonus and should be even more encouraging.

Check the current business and marketing literature for up-to-date trends. Faith Popcorn's books, *The Popcorn Report* and *Clicking: 16 Trends to Future Fit Your Life, Your Work, and Your Business*, and John Naisbitt's books, *Megatrends* and *Megatrends 2000*, are good starting points.

Megatrends was one of the first books to identify major trends. Many of these still apply. If your business is consistent with them, your chances for success expand.

Naisbitt's ten megatrends are

1. Although we continue to think we live in an industrial society, we have changed to an economy based on the creation and distribution of information.

2. We are moving in the dual directions of "high tech" and "high touch," matching each new technology with a compensatory human response.

3. No longer do we have the luxury of operating within an isolated, self-sufficient, national economic system; we now must acknowledge that we are part of a global economy.

4. We are restructuring from a society run by short-term considerations and rewards in favor of dealing with things over a much longer time frame.

5. In cities and states, in small organizations and subdivisions, we have rediscovered the ability to act

innovatively and to achieve results—starting from the bottom and moving to the top.

6. We are shifting from institutional help to more self-reliance in our lives.

7. We are discovering that the framework of representative democracy has become obsolete in an era of instantaneously shared information.

8. We are giving up our dependence on hierarchical structures in favor of informal networks.

9. More Americans are living in the South and West, leaving behind the old industrial cities of the North.

10. From a narrow either/or society with a limited range of personal choices, we are exploding into a freewheeling multiple-option society.

(Reprinted by permission of Warner Books, Inc., New York, U.S.A., from Megatrends, *by John Naisbitt, copyright © 1982. All rights reserved.)*

Trends will change over the years, but the process of analyzing your business as *on trend* or *off trend* remains. Apply it to your business. Update and personalize the listed trends, and use your own critical analysis and judgment to coincide with the current times.

Think through your ideas carefully before going forward. Get outside opinions, but don't be discouraged by negative comments if you objectively and honestly believe in the business or product. Weigh the pros and cons, sleep on any substantial ideas before taking action, and minimize your downside risk.

IDEA CHECKLISTS

Use these three checklists to analyze your business and product ideas:

Primary Criteria

✔ Is it effective? (Does it work?)
✔ Is it efficient? (Is it an improvement over status quo?)
✔ Is it compatible with human nature?
✔ Is it compatible with your goals?
✔ Is the timing right?
✔ Is it feasible? (Can you do it, and is it worth it?)
✔ Is it simple?

Value Engineering Principle

✓ What is it?
✓ What does it do?
✓ What does it cost?
✓ What else will do the job?
✓ What does that cost?

US Navy Checklist

✓ Will it increase production—or improve quality?
✓ Is it a more efficient utilization of staff?
✓ Does it improve methods of operation, maintenance, or construction?
✓ Is it an improvement over the present tools and machinery?
✓ Does it improve safety?
✓ Does it prevent waste or conserve materials?
✓ Does it eliminate unnecessary work?
✓ Does it reduce costs?
✓ Does it improve present methods?
✓ Will it improve working conditions?

Maintain the proper perspective in all this. You need to love your work, be an expert in it, and have some experience and education related to it. You must also ensure that there is a market for what you sell. You need a sustainable competitive advantage over others in the same market.

People often debate the major causes of business failure. The following list from a Dun & Bradstreet survey is a good summary of specific causes:

DEFICIENCY	PERCENTAGE OF FAILURES
Inadequate sales	39.0
Competitive weakness	21.2
Excessive operating expenses	11.2
Collection difficulties	9.3
Inventory difficulties	4.2
Excessive fixed assets	3.6
Neglect	2.8
Poor location	2.6
Disaster	1.4
Fraud	1.2
Other	1.4
Reason unknown	2.1

Condensing the findings in the list, the two major reasons for business failure are

➠ Inadequate market research before starting the business

➠ Poor planning and management

Don't let these problems defeat you. Investigate, plan, and implement on paper before going forward.

How long will you last in your business? If you are curious, check the following list compiled by the U.S. Department of Labor:

OCCUPATION	MEDIAN TENURE (YEARS)
Barbers	24.8
Farmers	21.1
Pilots	14.0
Civil engineers	13.0
Pharmacists	11.8
Chemists	11.1
Electricians	11.0
Physicians	10.7
Plumbers	10.4
Practical nurses	10.3
Lawyers	10.1
Truck drivers	10.1
Registered nurses	9.3
Managers and administrators	9.1
Personnel managers	9.0
Industrial engineers	8.9
Office supervisors	8.6
Sheriffs	8.6
Financial managers	8.4
Psychologists	8.4
Insurance salespeople	8.1
Carpenters	8.0
Musicians	7.9
Lab technicians	7.7
Purchasing managers	7.7
Accountants	7.6
Data processing equipment repairers	7.2
Health managers	7.2
Mail carriers	7.0
Management analysts	7.0
Computer systems analysts	6.6
Actors and directors	6.3
Real estate salespeople	6.0
Reporters and editors	6.0

OCCUPATION	MEDIAN TENURE (YEARS)
Teachers	5.9
Physician assistants	5.8
Public relations personnel	5.5
Financial products salespeople	5.4
Insurance adjusters and investigators	5.3
Physical therapists	5.2
Advertising salespeople	5.1
General salespeople	4.9
Computer operators	4.8
Computer programmers	4.8
Underwriters	4.8
Maids and housekeepers	4.6
Athletes	4.4
Bartenders	3.9
Car and boat salespeople	3.7
Receptionists	3.3
File clerks	2.5
Restaurant workers	1.7
Food counter clerks	1.5

CHAPTER 2
ACTION ITEMS

Finding and Evaluating Business Ideas

1. Uncover two possible business ideas this week as you go through your daily routine with your eyes wide open.

2. Evaluate your current business idea by asking yourself the four key questions. How did you score?

3. Pick ten current trends and run your business through the analysis. How did you score?

CHAPTER 3

Business Start-up Options

Start from scratch, buy a business, or buy a franchise? Once you decide to start a business and have a good idea of what kind of business, you have these three basic start-up options. Each has advantages and disadvantages. This chapter highlights many of these factors. Analyze and weigh the factors, and then make a final decision.

STARTING A BUSINESS

Most entrepreneurs start their businesses from scratch. Why is this so? Many do not even consider the two other options.

Here are a few of the most common advantages to starting your business from scratch:

- You can create a business, image, and reputation that reflects your personality.
- It gives you the opportunity to provide a unique service or product to the market.
- Customer contacts and relationships are new. There is no prior ill will.
- You can evaluate and choose new suppliers.
- You can evaluate and choose new employees.

- You can identify and acquire or lease an optimum location.
- No equipment, supplies, or inventory exist, so you can choose exactly what you want.
- You can develop and nurture new credit and banking relationships.

On the other hand, be aware of these disadvantages:

- Starting a business is riskier than buying an existing business.
- Starting and organizing a new business takes more time and energy than buying an existing business.
- Capital and credit may be more difficult to obtain because of lack of history and experience.
- It may take time to develop a solid customer base.
- You may need supplemental income in the early years, until the business becomes profitable.
- You are less sure of the marketability of your product or service.
- Talented and experienced employees may be difficult to obtain and compensate adequately.
- Costs are more difficult to estimate.

BUYING A BUSINESS

Buying an existing business might be the way for you to go. Even if you have clearly decided to start a business from scratch, you can learn a great deal by investigating and analyzing similar businesses for sale. The more information you can obtain, the more businesses you look at, and the more questions you ask, the more likely your start-up will be successful. Take the time to search. You may even find a gem.

The major advantages of buying an existing business are

- You can buy at a bargain price and bargain terms because the owner is often eager to sell.
- You can inherit proven inventory, supplies, equipment, and a facility at a bargain price.
- You can inherit good employees and loyal customers.

- You can be the beneficiary of goodwill and a positive reputation.
- There is less risk because the business has a track record.
- You can be profitable sooner.
- You can obtain a good proven location.
- You can save time by obtaining everything in one transaction.
- You can take advantage of established credit and supplier relationships.
- The financial records of the business can be a valuable starting point in running and growing the business.
- The seller may be available for valuable future assistance.
- You eliminate one competitor.

The major disadvantages of buying an existing business are

- The price may be too high.
- The business or owner may have a bad reputation.
- The personality and decor of the business may not reflect your tastes.
- You may inherit incompetent or inflexible employees.
- The business may be in a poor location or facility.
- You may inherit antiquated or obsolete inventory, fixtures, and equipment.
- The existing policies and procedures may be ineffective.
- You may inherit inappropriate customers or be unable to retain the valuable customers.
- You may not get along well with the existing landlord.
- You may be liable for contracts entered into by the prior owner.
- There may be some hidden debts and liabilities that unexpectedly show up later.
- The owner may take the customer base and goodwill to a new business or location.

Where do you find businesses for sale? Here are a few sources to consider:

- Check the "Business Opportunity" ads in your local Sunday newspaper and your local business or legal newspaper.
- Check the classified ads in the *Wall Street Journal.*
- Check the classified ads in trade and industry magazines.
- Contact real estate brokers and business brokers.
- Visit or call your local chamber of commerce. They may maintain lists or may know of interested sellers.
- Check with the SBA and other federal or state agencies that may know of businesses for sale.
- Talk to trade sources such as suppliers, distributors, manufacturers, and trade associations.
- Check with attorneys, accountants, bankers, friends, and acquaintances. Let them know that you are looking for a business opportunity.
- Contact business owners directly and ask whether they, or someone they know, wants to sell.
- Keep an eye open for opportunities that suggest a business may be for sale. Examples include death, divorce, illness, bankruptcy, and co-owner disagreements.

What factors should you consider before buying a business? Here are some ideas:

Personal Criteria

Identify your personal goals for purchasing the business. Will the business you are considering match these goals?

Think about your expertise. What are your strengths and weaknesses? Do they complement the venture? Will your knowledge and skills be of help in operating the business?

Consider your lifestyle. Does this business fit your status and image needs?

Decide about location. Is the location convenient for you? Does it have enough traffic flow? Is the location convenient to your target customers? What is the history behind the location?

Look at the surroundings and physical conditions. Do you need to remodel? What are the estimated costs?

Consider your financial needs. How much money do you want to make? How much money will you need to purchase the business?

Business Criteria

Obtain past and projected profit and sales figures. Ask for the past three to five years of audited financial statements, if they have them. Have your accountant review them.

Review the business's operating ratios. How do they compare with industry ratios from Robert Morris Associates' Annual Statement Studies or from Dun & Bradstreet's Key Business Ratios? Ask the owner to explain any significant deviations.

Obtain a list of all assets and liabilities. Examine the age and condition of inventory, equipment, and other assets. Evaluate debts and other liabilities. Are there any pending legal actions? Is product liability a concern? Analyze the number, amount, and ages of the receivables. How many did they write off as uncollectible in the past three years?

Review the tax returns of the past three to five years. Obtain income tax, sales tax, and payroll tax returns. Have your accountant review them. Compare them for consistency with each other and with the financial statements. If you doubt that these are the filed returns, obtain written authorization from the seller to obtain copies directly from the taxing agency.

Obtain copies of all current contracts, including leases, loans, supplier and customer agreements, and insurance policies. Check the OSHA requirements and compliance record. Can you and do you want to take over these obligations? Review all legal issues with your attorney.

Review corporate minutes. If the entity is a corporation, obtain copies of all relevant corporate documents to review.

Determine the value and legal protection of names, logos, trademarks, patents, and copyrights that are necessary for continued business success.

Run necessary background and credit checks. Dun & Bradstreet's credit reports, tax and lien liability searches, litigation searches, and a Better Business Bureau report are a good start.

Assess the current staff. If there are current employees, check their personnel files and interview them individually. Analyze compensation, skills, training, fringe benefits, union obligations, and turnover.

Evaluate local economic and political conditions. What are the industry trends for this business? Is the market increasing or decreasing? What is the growth potential? What is the competitive environment?

Meet with customers. Determine their level of satisfaction with the business. Talk to walk-in customers and former customers.

Deal with a cooperative seller. Will the seller be willing to assist with an orderly transition? If you don't get along with the seller, or if the seller is reluctant to disclose all the information you request, be concerned. Don't be afraid to walk away from the deal. There are many more opportunities out there.

Good price and good terms are essential when you finally decide to buy. Knowing the seller's motivation is imperative for you to negotiate the best deal.

Why do people sell businesses? The reason they volunteer is often not the real underlying reason. Remember that the seller wants to paint a bright picture to obtain the best price and terms. However, people don't generally sell businesses that are doing well, have a bright future, and are enjoyable to own and run. Your job is to determine the real reason for selling before you go too far in the transaction. It will put you in a much stronger bargaining position. Recognize that the seller has only one business to sell. You have many possible businesses you could buy, if you even do buy. You should be in the power negotiating position.

Here are some of the most common reasons owners claim that they are selling the business:

- Owner wants to retire.
- Owner wants to collect the winnings and enjoy them.
- Owner wants to live somewhere else.

- Illness is pressuring the owner to leave the business.
- Owner needs to deal with estate and inheritance problems.
- Owner is not happy with the line of business.
- There is a dispute between co-owners.

Here are some reasons owners are less likely to volunteer:

- Owner has family pressures.
- Owner has marital problems.
- Owner sees a better business opportunity.
- Owner dislikes coping with unions, regulations, taxes, consumer groups, stockholders, inflation, or insurance costs.
- Company needs more financing than the owner can raise.
- The market for what the company sells is currently depressed.
- Company is losing money for reasons the owner cannot diagnose.

Here are some reasons owners will rarely volunteer:

- Bigger companies are squeezing out smaller companies.
- New zoning laws are too restrictive.
- Competitors are moving in with more effective products or methods.
- Union settlements are cutting into profit.
- Owner wants to start a competitive firm with greater potential.
- Plant has become worn out or obsolete.
- New government regulations are too expensive.
- Supply sources have become restricted or eliminated.
- Location is becoming obsolete.
- Product or service the company sells is becoming obsolete.
- Franchise is being canceled.
- Company needs more cash than operations can justify.
- Key employees are leaving, perhaps as competitors.
- There is an impending threat of a major lawsuit.

- Major customer returns are likely from previous sales.
- There is a backlog with major built-in losses.

The key for you is to determine the real reason or reasons. Some reasons may necessitate walking away from the deal. Others may signify a great opportunity. You will decide, but do so knowing all the facts.

What is the value of a business? Entire books describe valuation techniques in great detail. This section discusses highlights of the major techniques. There is no single correct approach to valuation. Professional business appraisers will apply several techniques. However, what a business eventually sells for is often dependent on the buyer's and seller's subjective views and negotiating skills.

The three generally accepted methods of valuation are

1. **Balance sheet method:** Assets minus liabilities give a value to the business. Variations include pure book value (historic cost), adjusted book value (fair market value), and liquidation value (immediate sale).

2. **Income statement method:** Capitalize earnings or sales with a chosen capitalization rate. Make decisions on what years to average for earnings or sales, what adjustments to make to earnings (taxes, interest, depreciation, owner compensation), and what growth and capitalization rates to use.

3. **Discounted cash flow:** Project cash flow of the business into the future, choosing an appropriate discount rate, and discounting the cash flows back to today's present value.

You need accurate data from the seller to perform a proper analysis. You may want to hire an accountant or a specialized business appraiser to perform a detailed analysis. However, use the following suggestions to obtain an approximate value.

Use the liquidation value as the floor, or low end, of what a business is worth. Use the adjusted book value based on fair market value of assets as a quick gauge of reasonable value.

Use the capitalized earnings method to get your best idea of the most you would pay. Be sure to adjust the reported earnings appropriately before applying a capitalization rate. At the very least, factor in a reasonable cost for managing the business (even if you plan to do it yourself). Also factor in an annual replacement fund contribution for equipment. Carefully analyze all other expenses in the financial data. Some may be too high. (For example, the owner may have included personal expenses of the business.) Others may be too low or missing altogether. Your goal is to develop the projected future income statement, but without adding in the extra value or sales increase that you hope to inject.

Capitalization rates are the return you want to earn on your investment. Recognize that this should be in addition to the compensation you receive for actually working in the business. That's why it is important to factor in such compensation as an operating expense when doing the business valuation.

Running your own business is risky with a large downside. You can easily and very securely earn 5 percent to 6 percent with bank or large corporate obligations. You can probably earn 10 percent to 15 percent with growth stocks, trust deeds, and other slightly riskier investments. Therefore, it only makes sense to earn a minimum of 15 percent and more likely 25 percent to 35 percent, on a business opportunity.

Assume that a business earns $50,000 per year after your adjustments. If you want a 25 percent return (capitalization rate), that corresponds with a multiplier of four. (Four times earnings gives you the price that would earn a 25 percent return on your investment.) Therefore, with these assumptions, you value the business at $200,000.

Typical multiples for private businesses range from three to eight. Lower multiples (and correspondingly higher capitalization rates) produce lower valuations. Factors to consider are risk, growth, history, and glamour. You would likely value most small private businesses at four to five times their adjusted earnings. This equates to a 20 percent to 25 percent return.

Recognize that many businesses for sale, after you make the necessary adjustments, are worth little or nothing. The seller's asking price is often much higher than reality and careful analysis justify.

Now that you have found a great business at a great price, don't forget the terms. They can often be more important than the actual price. Generally you want to put down as little as possible and have the owner carry the balance at a low interest rate for as long as possible. This serves two purposes. One, you improve your cash flow position. Two, if there are any future problems that you feel the seller did not disclose and should be liable for, you have substantial leverage since you are still paying the seller.

Locate a good lawyer and a good escrow company to help you close the transaction. If you and your lawyer can draft the contract, do it. If the seller drafts the contract, have your lawyer carefully review it.

Here are some typical provisions to include:

- Names and addresses of all parties and their spouses
- Total price
- Complete detailed description of all tangible and intangible assets with price allocation
- Payment terms with interest rate and due dates
- Adjustments to make at closing
- Contracts and liabilities the purchaser assumes
- Seller's warranties as to ownership, liabilities, disclosure, and authority
- Duration of seller's warranties
- Conduct of business up to closing
- Buyer's rights as to cancellation of contract
- Noncompetition agreement by seller detailing type, time, and location
- Employment or consulting agreement with seller
- Responsibility for closing details
- Indemnification of buyer by seller
- Broker compensation payment
- Arbitration agreement and attorneys' fee agreement
- Approval of contract with all parties signing and indicating their signing capacity

BUYING A FRANCHISE

Should you buy a business franchise? Franchise ownership has aspects of both owning your own business and working as an employee for someone else. It may be the perfect opportunity for someone who wants to own a business but needs a little more structure and a little less risk. Franchises are most appropriate for people who have considerable financial resources to pursue their ideas.

Here are some of the advantages:

- A proven and tested successful concept reduces your risk of failure.
- You often have a turnkey operation in a total package.
- You have standardized products and systems that work.
- You have standardized financial and accounting systems in place.
- You have collective buying power.
- The franchisor often provides ongoing supervision, consulting, and training.
- You benefit from national and local advertising programs.
- The franchisor often provides useful advertising and marketing materials.
- The franchisor often provides uniform packaging.
- You benefit from ongoing research and development of new products, new variations, new ideas, and new systems.
- The franchisor may provide financial assistance in purchasing the franchise and necessary equipment.
- You receive assistance in proper site selection.
- You have detailed operations manuals.
- The franchisor may provide sales and marketing assistance.
- You are likely to receive planning and forecasting data and assistance.

Disadvantages include the following:

- You lose substantial control in making major business decisions by being subject to franchisor guidelines.
- Franchises are often expensive to purchase.
- You are often liable for a continuing royalty and advertising fee.
- Strict binding franchise agreements favor the franchisor.
- The franchisor's problems will reflect on your business.

- The franchisor may restrict your choice of suppliers, products, or services.
- You may have a limited territory and may be subject to another franchise opening within your territory.
- It may be very difficult and expensive to sell or transfer ownership of the franchise.
- You may not be able to exercise your full creativity and uniqueness.

At your earliest opportunity, obtain a copy of the franchise's Uniform Franchise Offering Circular (UFOC) required by the Federal Trade Commission (FTC). The franchisor must deliver this disclosure document to you at the first personal contact. However, try to obtain it sooner. It will give you a wealth of information in a consistent and organized format.

The franchisor must fully disclose information in the following twenty categories:

1. Identifying information as to franchisor
2. Business experience of franchisor's directors and executive officers
3. Business experience of the franchisor
4. Litigation history
5. Bankruptcy history
6. Description of the franchise
7. Initial funds required from the franchisee
8. Recurring funds required from the franchisee
9. Affiliated persons with whom the franchisor requires or advises the franchisee to do business
10. Obligations to purchase
11. Revenues received by the franchisor in consideration of the purchase
12. Financing arrangements
13. Restriction of sales
14. Personal participation required of the franchisee in the operation of the franchise
15. Termination, cancellation, and renewal of the franchise
16. Statistical information concerning the number of franchises and company-owned outlets
17. Site selection
18. Training programs

19. Public figure involvement in the franchise
20. Financial information concerning the franchisor

Review the UFOC carefully, and highlight the areas where you want more information. Visit and talk with current and former franchisees. Even if you don't purchase the franchise, you will obtain valuable information about the industry, what works, and what doesn't work. This knowledge will dramatically increase your own chances for success.

Here is a helpful franchise evaluation checklist to assist you:

The Franchise Opportunity Itself

✓ Did your lawyer approve the franchise contract after he studied it?

✓ Does the franchise call upon you to take any steps that are unwise or illegal in your state, county, or city?

✓ Does the franchise give you an exclusive territory for the length of the franchise, or can the franchisor sell a second or third franchise in your territory?

✓ Does the franchisor do business with other franchisors that handle similar merchandise or services?

✓ If the answer to the last question is yes, what is your protection against this second franchisor organization?

✓ Under what circumstances and at what cost can you pull out of the franchise contract?

✓ If you sell your franchise, will the purchaser pay you for your goodwill, or will you lose the value you have built into the business?

The Franchisor

✓ How many years has the franchisor been in business?

✓ Does the franchisor have a reputation for honesty and fair dealing among the local entrepreneurs holding its franchise?

✓ Has the franchisor shown you any certified figures indicating exact net profits of one or more existing franchises? Have you checked with the franchisee?

✓ Will the franchisor help you with management training programs, employee training programs, public relations programs, merchandising ideas, or financing ideas?

✓ Will the franchisor help you find a good location for your franchise?

✓ Does the franchisor have adequate financing to carry out its stated plan of financial help and expansion?

✓ Is the franchisor a one-person company or a larger company with a trained and experienced management team?

✓ Exactly what can the franchisor do for you that you cannot do for yourself?

✓ Has the franchisor investigated you carefully enough to assure itself that you can successfully operate a franchise at a profit for both of you?

The Franchisee (You!)

✓ How much equity capital will you need to buy the franchise and operate it until your sales revenues exceed your expenses?

✓ Where are you going to get the equity capital you need?

✓ Will you give up some independence of action to get the advantages offered by the franchise?

✓ Are you confident you have the ability, training, and experience to work smoothly and profitably with the franchisor, your employees, and your customers?

✓ Are you ready to spend much or all of the rest of your business life with this franchisor, offering its product or service to your public?

The Market

- ✓ Have you thoroughly researched the product or service market and its pricing?
- ✓ Will the population in your territory increase, remain static, or decrease over the next five years?
- ✓ Will the demand for the product or service you are considering be greater, about the same, or less in five years?
- ✓ What competition exists in your territory for the product or service from both franchise and nonfranchise firms?

CHAPTER 3
ACTION ITEMS

Business Start-up Options

1. Determine whether you will start a business, buy a business, or buy a franchise. Explain your rationale.

2. Review the business opportunities in the classified ad section of your local business newspaper.

3. Obtain and review a UFOC for a business closely related to your idea.

CHAPTER 4

Developing Your Business Plan

Success is the progressive journey toward predetermined worthwhile goals. Those goals should be specific, challenging, and in writing, with a projected time frame for accomplishment. These rules apply to life goals as well as business goals.

This chapter explains the need for a written business plan and the basic components of a successful plan. It ends with some tips to make your business plan even more impressive to bankers and investors.

WHY WRITE A BUSINESS PLAN?

Why do you need a written business plan? One important reason is that lenders and outside investors usually require it. However, the main use for a written plan is to help you. Make your mistakes on paper and learn about potential problems before they occur. You can determine whether or not the business should proceed. The plan can help you improve your concept, and it forces you to think through all aspects of the business before proceeding. A well-researched business plan can save substantial time, money, and stress.

A preliminary step to a complete business plan is a feasibility analysis. This is particularly valuable if you are looking at several opportunities, and you want to compare the potential of each before making a final decision. Feasibility studies, either formal or informal, assist you in determining whether or not your idea is worth pursuing. Your findings indicate whether you need to complete a comprehensive business plan.

If you performed the self-analysis and the idea-analysis suggested in chapters 1 and 2, you have already completed a simple type of feasibility analysis. However, there are a few more issues you should cover.

A good feasibility study should answer the following questions:

- Do you truly want to own your own business?
- Will this business give you the tangible and intangible benefits you and your family desire from a business?
- What are the major business risks?
- What is the market for this business? What is its future?
- What are the preliminary sales and income forecasts for the business? What data and research do you have to back up the forecasts?
- What is the competition? What do you offer that is superior?
- What are the start-up and operating expenses? Where will you get the funding?

If you are looking at several business opportunities, assign a numerical rating to the various factors and prepare a weighted comparison. This will help you make a more objective decision.

Once you have a tentative go-ahead for a business idea, it's time to prepare the more complete business plan. You can probably use much of the data and information previously compiled for your feasibility study.

BUSINESS PLAN COMPONENTS

Many entrepreneurs dread and avoid writing business plans. Anything that takes substantial effort and time and must be in writing is a major challenge for most. School book reports and term papers were similar projects with similar results for many.

You probably procrastinated on those assignments. However, you most likely felt great satisfaction and a sense of accomplishment when you finally completed them. Think about all the aggravation and stress that your procrastination caused. A different mental approach to the whole process could have dramatically improved the situation.

Unless you need outside debt or equity financing, no one is forcing you to write a business plan. You must convince yourself that the benefits outweigh and justify the costs.

Most business authors and consultants have their own suggested format for a business plan. In a way, it's similar to writing a resume in that there are numerous formats on how to express the information. However, most experts agree that you should include certain major items. Prepare an introduction and a concise summary. Separate sections on marketing, management, and finances are standard.

Browse through the business planning books at bookstores and libraries. Find an author and a format that is comfortable for you. Some books and methods are quite sophisticated, and others are very informal. Review the many selections. You will learn a lot from this step alone.

Computers also can be useful in preparing your business plan. Word processing and spreadsheet analysis software make writing the plan and producing the necessary financial calculations and analysis less burdensome. The physical presentation is also much more professional.

Start the process even if you don't have access to the recommended hardware or software. Much of the work that goes into the plan requires research. You can defer or delegate final presentation and financial calculations. It's important to start and work on your plan regularly with definite and specific short-term and long-term goals, each with a timeline.

Here are some brief descriptions of three best-selling business planning books. All three are easy and enjoyable to read, and they provide specific examples of completed business plans. They also have inexpensive software packages to assist in the plan preparation. The publishers regularly update each book.

➧ *How to Write a Business Plan*, by Mike McKeever, published by Nolo Press, goes through the process step-by-step with many start-up business examples. It includes fill-in-the-blank financial forms and several sample business plans.

➤ *The Business Planning Guide*, by David H. Bangs, Jr., published by Upstart Publishing Company, follows an actual start-up business through each stage of the analysis and writing process.

➤ *Business Plan Pro*, by Tim Berry, published by Palo Alto Software, is primarily an integrated software program for completing all steps of the plan on the computer. However, the manual itself is an excellent guide to writing an effective plan.

All three of the publishers listed above have additional books and software relevant to small business that may be helpful to you. Call each and obtain their current catalog of products. Contact information as of the date of this publication:

- Nolo Press: (800) 992-6656; Internet: http://www.nolo.com
- Upstart Publishing Company: (800) 235-8866
- Palo Alto Software: (800) 229-7526; Internet: http://www.pasware.com

Each of the plans uses a slightly different format. Remember, however, that the format is much less important than the substance and the process of researching and writing. Cover all the major steps and you will have a good plan.

This section describes the *Business Plan Pro* manual text, tables, and charts. They serve as excellent guides and examples because they are simple, concise, and fully integrated in one software product. You can add, delete, or alter sections to fit any situation. It's an excellent program for the excited, but confused, new entrepreneur. Other good planning books and software cover the same major points and issues.

Later chapters will cover many of the specifics discussed in the formal plan. View the big picture in this chapter before addressing individual items.

Here is a suggested outline of the text along with some brief comments on what to include:

1.0   Executive Summary

The executive summary is the doorway to the rest of the plan. Get it right or your target readers will not proceed. The best length is a single page. Emphasize the main points of your plan and keep it brief.

1.1 Objectives

Objectives are business goals. Set your market share objectives, sales objectives, and profit objectives. Companies need to set objectives and plan to achieve them. Ensure that they are concrete and measurable. State specific goals such as achieving a given level of sales or profits, a percentage of gross margin, a growth rate, or a market share. Don't use generalities like "being the best" or "growing rapidly."

1.2 Mission

A mission should be a one-paragraph summary of a company's purpose, values, and goals. Developing a mission statement is often a valuable initial step in developing a business plan. Use it to define your business.

1.3 Keys to Success

What are the keys to success in this business? Focus here on no more than three or four of the most important factors. The true keys to success will be different for every business. Think about major points, rather than details. For example, the keys to success of a computer store might be reliable service, competitive pricing, and convenient parking.

2.0 Company

Use this first paragraph to summarize the company information from the following topic headings. Be brief. Explain what your company sells, through what channels, and to whom.

2.1 Ownership

In this paragraph, describe the ownership of the company. Is it a corporation? Publicly traded? Privately owned? Partnership or sole proprietorship?

2.2 History

For ongoing companies: When was the company founded? By whom? For what purpose? How has it progressed since its founding? When did it move to new locations, expand product lines, or otherwise change substantially? Remember to include information about sales, products, markets, and how they have changed over time.

2.3 Start-up Plan

Use this section for start-up businesses with no company history. Use this section to describe your start-up plan. How much money do you need for initial expenses and beginning assets? How will you finance this?

2.4 Business Concept

Use this section to answer the important question: What business am I in? Focus on the most important elements of your business. What are you selling? To whom do you sell? For example, restaurants normally sell service and convenience much more than they sell food. Chocolate makers sell oral satisfaction as much as they sell candy. Some auto makers sell safety, some sell status and prestige, and some sell transportation.

2.5 Facilities

Briefly describe the offices and locations of your company. Explain the nature and function of each. Specify the square footage, lease arrangements, and other relevant data.

3.0 Product or Service

This first paragraph is a summary of the rest of this section. It should be a clear and concise single paragraph. You should be able to merge it into the executive summary page. What do you sell, and to whom?

3.1 Description

List and describe the products and services your company sells. Think in terms of products and customer needs. How do the products fill the market demand? How do they supply what the customers need?

3.2 Comparison

Describe the important competitive features of your products and services. Why do people buy yours instead of others? Do you sell better features, better price, better quality, better service, or some other factor? Prepare a matrix comparing your product to competitors' products.

3.3 Sales Literature

Include copies of advertisements, brochures, direct mail pieces, catalogs, and technical specifications.

3.4 Sourcing

Explain product sourcing and the cost of fulfilling your service. Manufacturers and assemblers should present spreadsheet output showing standard costs and overhead. Distributors should present discount and margin structures. Service companies should present costs of fulfilling service obligations.

3.5 Technology

The product is based on what technology? How is the product technology protected? (patent, copyright, trademark, trade secret)

3.6 Future

Present an outlook for future products or services. Do you have a long-term product strategy? How do you develop products? Is there a relationship between market segments, market demand, market needs, and product development?

4.0   Market Analysis

The first paragraph is a summary of information from the following topics. Highlight the key elements, including market size and growth rate projections.

4.1 Market Segmentation

The market segmentation concept is crucial to market assessment and marketing strategy. Divide the market into workable market segments—age, income, product type, geography, buying patterns, customer needs, or other classifications. Define your terms, and define your market.

4.2 Industry Analysis

This section sets the scene for the market forecast that follows. Use secondary research sources to produce general industry information that will serve as important background material.

4.3 Market Analysis

Use the text to summarize and point out highlights of your detailed market analysis. Examine your total potential customers, focusing on different customer segments.

5.0   Strategy and Implementation

In this first paragraph, explain the heart of your sales and marketing strategy. What is your overall strategic thrust—new technology, new products, new product features, better marketing, lower price, better distribution, better service, and so forth? Choose one of these, not all.

5.1 Marketing Strategy

When describing strategy, emphasize what makes your company special. For example, your marketing strategy might focus on a specific market segment or special ways to distribute the product. It might focus on new products that are new solutions to existing problems or on new ways to promote products or services. What will you do better than anybody else? Strategy depends more on what you leave out than what you include—focus and emphasis are extremely important.

5.2 Sales Strategy

How do you sell? Retail, wholesale, discount, mail order, phone order? Do you maintain a sales force? How do you train and compensate salespeople? Include computer spreadsheet output on sales strategy.

5.3 Strategic Alliances

Explain co-marketing, co-development, commission, and cooperative arrangements. Does any other company control your fate? Can you link your promotion or distribution strategies to other companies in a way that improves your company's position?

5.4 Service

This category is important for some businesses. Is it for yours? How do you propose to service the products you sell?

5.5 Milestones

This ought to be the most important section of the entire business plan. Use milestones to fix specific dates and objectives for all of the programs included in the plan. This is where what might be time wasted in theoretical planning and long-term strategy becomes time invested in concrete planning and implementation. The benefit of milestones is follow-up. Business plan milestones are commitments to tasks, goals, and deadlines.

6.0   Organization

Use the first paragraph as a summary. Include the number of employees that are in the company, and how many members are in the management team. How many are founders of the company?

6.1 Organizational Structure

Use this section to include an organization chart. If possible with your software, draw the chart in a drawing program and link it back into this spot. In the text, list the positions and the responsibilities of each management position.

6.2 Management Team

List the most important members of the management team. Include summaries of their backgrounds and experience. Describe management functions within the company. Note that the following section discusses weaknesses and gaps of the management team.

6.3 Management Team Gaps

Specify where the team is weak and where there are holes. Specify how you will fill the holes. Many companies lack a complete team. They often have personnel shortages in marketing and manufacturing departments.

6.4 Personnel Plan

Use a Personnel Plan table to prepare more detailed information on projected growth of personnel.

6.5 Other Considerations

Applicability depends on your company. Answer these questions: Do any managers or employees have noncompetition agreements with competitors? Who is on your board of directors? What do the members contribute to the business? Who are your major stockholders? What is their role with the management of the business?

7.0 Financial Plan

Show the most important highlights: projected cash flow and net profit for the next three years, return on investment, and internal rate of return.

7.1 Assumptions

Use this section to discuss important assumptions, including those covered in the General Assumptions table, which is discussed on page 64. Explain how key assumptions have affected your financial projections.

7.2 Key Financial Indicators

Refer to the Benchmarks chart (discussed on page 65), which contains indicator values for the most important financial ratios.

It automatically compares past results and projected results for ongoing companies, and year-by-year projections for start-ups. Use the Benchmarks chart to explain your key financial guidelines.

7.3 Break-even Analysis

Use the text to discuss the break-even assumptions for fixed costs, variable costs, and average pricing. Print a Break-even chart based on the data from the Break-even Analysis table.

7.4 Profit and Loss

Briefly explain highlights from the Profit and Loss table, such as growth rates or profitability.

7.5 Cash Flow

Briefly explain the main points of the Cash Flow table. Prepare the projected Cash Flow table and the related Cash chart.

7.6 Balance Sheet

Include some highlights here. Chapter 18 discusses the balance sheet in more detail.

7.7 Business Ratios

Discuss the most important business ratios. Chapter 18 discusses ratios in more detail.

These are the suggested Business Plan Tables:

General Assumptions. This table sets general assumptions used by many of the other tables. It includes interest rates, collection days, payment days, tax rate, cash expense percent, credit sales percent, and payroll tax percent.

Break-even Analysis. This table shows break-even point calculations.

Market Analysis. This table shows potential customers in different market segments.

Profit and Loss. This table shows your profit and loss projection. The structure depends on type of business organization.

Cash Flow. This table shows your cash receipts and disbursements projection.

Balance Sheet. This table shows assets, liabilities, and capital. The structure depends on type of business organization.

Milestones. This lists specific implementation milestones. It includes responsible person, budget, and date of completion.

Ratios. This table shows calculations of more than a dozen key business ratios.

Sales Forecast. This table projects sales and costs of sales.

Personnel Plan. This table shows payroll costs, including salaries and payroll burden.

Start-up. This table shows the start-up expenses and beginning balances for start-up companies.

Past Performance. This table lists the most important past financial data of ongoing companies.

These are the suggested Business Plan Charts:

Cash. This chart's columns show cash balance and cash flow for the next twelve months.

Highlights. This chart's columns show sales, gross margin, and earnings by year.

Benchmarks. This chart's columns show changes in key business indicators by year.

Sales Monthly. This chart's columns show sales for each of the first twelve months.

Sales by Year. This chart's columns show sales by year.

Break-even. This line chart shows profits or losses at different sales levels, crossing zero at break-even point.

Markets. This pie chart shows potential customers in different market segments.

Past (or Start-Up). This chart's columns show highlights of past results for ongoing companies and the start-up balances for start-ups.

FINE-TUNING TIPS

If you are using the business plan to obtain outside debt or equity financing, you need to fully support and document your analysis and conclusions. Make a very professional presentation.

Here are a few tips on adding the final touches and making sure the final plan is ready:

- Provide an executive summary and table of contents.
- Tab each section for easy reference.
- Utilize an attractive and professional looking cover or binder.
- Make sure the plan fits your need. It should not be too long, short, fancy, or plain.
- Use graphs, charts, diagrams, pictures, photographs, and other relevant visual aids to add interest and improve comprehension.
- Number and account for each copy of the plan, and indicate that the information is proprietary and confidential.
- Obtain independent review and recommendations of the plan from entrepreneurs, accountants, lawyers, bankers, and other carefully chosen third parties.
- Make it clear what you expect to accomplish in the business and what you want from the reader.
- Explain in both quantitative and qualitative terms the benefit to the user of the products or services.
- Present solid evidence of marketability.
- Explain and justify the product development and any manufacturing process along with associated costs.
- Document the financial projections and data, and ensure they are realistic and believable.
- Portray the management team as experienced and having complementary skills.
- Show investors how they will cash out in an appropriate time frame with capital appreciation.

CHAPTER 4
ACTION ITEMS

Developing Your Business Plan

1. Review several business plan books in your library or bookstore.

2. Review several business plans of actual companies.

3. Prepare an outline of your business plan and a draft of the executive summary.

CHAPTER 5

Finding Your Niche and Researching Your Market

Chocolate-chip cookies are the main product of a multimillion dollar retail empire called Mrs. Fields' Cookies. Who would have imagined a few years ago that such a small, seemingly unimportant, individual product could be the basis for an entire business, and later an entire industry? This is clearly the age of specialization, with successful companies better serving small identifiable markets with a specific product or service.

You can't be all things to all people, and you can't expect to serve everyone. Your business will have a much greater chance for success if you concentrate on a narrow market and strive to serve that market better and more efficiently than any competitor. Even if your targeted market is a very small portion of the total product market, you can be very successful. If you don't specialize, someone else likely will specialize. They will be better able to serve that segment. You may lose your competitive edge.

This chapter discusses your need to segment the broad market you are entering, target one segment, and position your product to best serve the chosen target. The chapter also highlights valuable marketing resources.

SEGMENTING AND TARGETING YOUR MARKET

Why are there hundreds of beverage varieties? Dozens of cola variations? Hundreds of automobile models? If the only requirement was to satisfy basic thirst and transportation needs, wouldn't one or two types each satisfy those needs?

Obviously, there is much more going on than mere satisfaction of basic thirst and transportation needs. Each of the variations is developed and marketed toward specific markets of consumers with identified wants, needs, and characteristics. Your market is likely no different.

Segmenting your market requires some careful research and analysis. It consists of taking the broad product or service market and dividing it into several homogeneous submarkets.

Identify segments using various techniques. Each broad product or service market lends itself to different approaches, but here's a simplified version that applies to many:

- Determine the broad product or service market. *Transportation* is an example.
- List all the potential customer wants and needs that the product or service can satisfy. Examples for the broad transportation market include safety, speed, status, economy, value, space, reliability, prestige, power, maneuverability, storage, hauling capacity, and comfort.
- Determine which of the identified wants and needs are unique to certain groups of similar people. Separate them into logical homogeneous submarkets. For example, safety is a major concern of a young family seeking transportation. The young affluent male is seeking power and prestige.
- Fine-tune the various submarkets and combine or divide them if appropriate.
- Estimate the market size of each.

Targeting your market consists of choosing one of the segments that you have identified, and going after that target with full force. Ignore the other segments. Let others go after them. Concentrate on satisfying your chosen segment better than anyone else.

There are times when you can go after two or more segments if you feel the markets are similar, or if you have the time and resources to develop separate strategies for each. However, more businesses make the mistake of trying to go after too much and trying to make everyone happy. They often try to be all things to all people. Fewer businesses make the mistake of trying to serve a market that is too narrow. Realize that you can become very successful and quite wealthy by serving a small segment of a broad market better than anyone else. As you learn and grow, it may make sense to later expand into related segments. However, don't lose that specialized niche or market that originally made you a success.

When choosing an appropriate segment to target, keep the following tips in mind:

- Make sure you can efficiently identify and measure the members of the chosen market.
- Make sure the segment is large enough to be profitable.
- Make sure the segment is economically reachable through a planned marketing program.
- Make sure the segment is responsive to a planned marketing program.
- Make sure the segment will be around for some time and will not change dramatically.

Once you have satisfactorily identified your target market, learn as much as you can about your typical targeted customer. You want to satisfy this person's needs better than anyone else. To do that, you need to research, study, and analyze your prospective customers. The more you know about them, the better you can serve them, and the more effectively and efficiently you can reach them.

What information should you obtain about your targeted customers? The section that follows lists the traditional variables. Identify as many relevant variables as possible. The more information you can find on these variables, the better. Not all will apply, but don't dismiss them without proper consideration.

Geographic and demographic variables are the most logical breakdowns. Psychographic and behavioristic variables are more subtle and more difficult to determine and measure. However, if such variables are available and relevant, they can be a gold mine of information.

TARGET MARKET VARIABLES WITH TYPICAL BREAKDOWNS

Geographic

Region: Pacific, Mountain, West North Central, West South Central, East North Central, East South Central, South Atlantic, Middle Atlantic, New England

County size: A (all counties in the twenty-five largest metropolitan areas), B (over 150,000 population), C (over 35,000 population), D (all remaining)

City or MSA (Metropolitan Statistical Area) size: Under 5,000; 5,000–19,999; 20,000–49,999;50,000–99,999; 100,000–249,999; 250,000–499,999; 500,000–999,999; 1,000,000–3,999,999; 4,000,000 and over

Other geographic measures: State, census tract, block numbering area, block group, Zip Code, Zip+4, postal delivery routes, block

Density: Urban, suburban, rural

Climate: Warm, cold

Demographic

Age: Under 6, 6–11, 12–19, 20–34, 35–49, 50–64, 65 and over

Gender: Male, female

Family size: 1–2, 3–4, 5 or more

Family life cycle: Early childhood (Birth–5); late childhood (6–12); early adolescence (13–15); late adolescence (16–18); young singles (19–24); young married (25–34); young divorced without children (28–34); young parents (25–34); young divorced with children (28–34); middle-aged married with children (35–44); middle-aged married without children (35–44); middle-aged divorced with children (35–44); later adulthood (45–54); soon-to-be-retired (55–64); already retired (65 and older)

Income: Under $10,000; $10,001–$20,000; $20,001–$30,000; $30,001–$40,000; $40,001–$60,000; $60,001–$100,000; $100,001 and over

Occupation: Professional, managerial, proprietor, office worker, skilled trade, technical, homemaker, general laborer, student, sales, farmer, supervisor, craftsperson, public official, retired, unemployed

Education: Less than 8 years, 9–11 years, high-school graduate, technical or vocational school, 1–2 years college, 3–4 years college, college graduate, graduate or professional degree

Religion: Catholic, Jewish, Protestant, other

Race: White, Black, Asian, Hispanic

Nationality: American, British, Chinese, French, German, Italian, Japanese, Latin American, Middle Eastern, Scandinavian, Spanish

Psychographic

Social class: Lower lowers, upper lowers, lower middles, upper middles, lower uppers, upper uppers

Lifestyle: Belongers, achievers, emulators, sexual preference, swingers

Personality: Compulsive, gregarious, authoritarian, ambitious, achieving, egotistical

Behavioristic

Purchase occasion: Regular occasion, special occasion

Benefits sought: Economy, convenience, prestige

User status: Nonuser, ex-user, potential user, first-time user, regular user

Usage rate: Light user, medium user, heavy user

Loyalty status: None, medium, strong, absolute

Readiness stage: Unaware, aware, informed, interested, desirous, intending to buy

Marketing factor sensitivity: Quality, price, service, advertising, sales promotion

Attitude toward product: Enthusiastic, positive, indifferent, negative, hostile

Start and maintain a comprehensive database of all your current and prospective customers from day one. Don't allow a potential customer to leave the business or hang up on the telephone without obtaining basic name, address, and phone information. For regular customers, and especially for your most important customers, obtain and catalog additional data. It will be helpful in your marketing, promotion, and customer service. In his informative and entertaining first book, *Swim with the Sharks without Being Eaten Alive*, author and successful executive Harvey Mackay lists the 66 items he wants to know about each customer. Use the Mackay 66™ as a starting point for the information you need. Add, delete, and change appropriately to meet your business needs.

POSITIONING AND DEVELOPING A POWERFUL USP

Position your product in the customer's mind and develop a powerful *unique selling proposition* (USP) that clearly explains and reinforces your company's benefits to that consumer. That's your next step!

Al Ries and Jack Trout emphasize the importance of each business creating a *position* with its products and services in the prospective customer's mind, in their landmark book, *Positioning: The Battle for Your Mind*. The *position* or *customer mind-set* you take should consider your company's strengths and weaknesses as well as the competition's strengths and weaknesses. That position can be as a leader, a follower, or numerous other positions. You can develop a successful business from a variety of positions. The important point is to intelligently analyze the market, your own business, and the competition. Develop a rational and consistent strategy after you complete your analysis.

Ries and Trout give numerous examples of both successful and unsuccessful positioning attempts. They describe possible strategies for positioning your business. Some of the case histories may apply to your situation.

Key factors in determining and developing the most effective position in the customer's mind are

- Careful identification and analysis of all primary and secondary competitors
- Determination of how consumers evaluate their options
- Determination of how competitors are perceived by consumers
- Identification of gaps in the various competitors' current positions
- Careful analysis of your unique abilities, qualities, or other factors

Your target market and the position you aim for in your customer's mind should assist in developing a powerful USP for your business. Your USP is crucial to your business identity and success. It is a differentiating and appealing idea that sets you and your business apart from the competition. You build your marketing and operational success upon your USP. It is the primary distinguishing advantage you hold out in all your marketing, advertising, and sales efforts.

Your USP should be *unique,* or at least perceived in the mind of the customer as unique. It should also be a *selling proposition.* You must believe the customer will make a buying decision based substantially on this factor.

Some businesses have several USPs, but it takes only one powerful one to make your business successful. Possibilities include the following:

- Highest quality
- Fastest service
- Lowest price
- Longer hours
- Widest selection
- Specialized selection
- Advice and assistance
- Convenience
- Longer warranty

Any of these and many more can form the basis for an effective USP. Be as specific as you can when defining your USP. *Quality* and *service* are terms used so often that they are almost meaningless. You need to add details and proof to back up the claims.

Examples of very powerful and successful USPs include

- Apple Computer's user-friendliness
- Volvo's safety record
- Nordstrom's impeccable service
- Blockbuster's large selection
- Federal Express's guaranteed overnight delivery

MARKETING RESEARCH AND RESOURCES

Proper market research is important to determine if there is a need and desire for your product and to find out the characteristics of the market. Good research can also assist in pricing, promotion, and distribution decisions. Market research consists of secondary research and primary research. Secondary research is the analysis of previously collected, organized, and printed data. Primary research is any original data and information you collect and analyze. Questionnaires, surveys, and other information-gathering methods are examples of primary research. Primary research is useful, but it can be costly and time-consuming. Thoroughly analyze all available secondary research data before you attempt primary research.

Before starting your research, be sure to identify your specific Standard Industrial Classification (SIC) code. SIC codes categorize much of the relevant secondary research information from government and trade sources. Find the four-digit SIC code for your business. If possible, determine the six-digit or eight-digit code that even more finely describes your business. The federal government publishes a *Standard Industrial Classification Manual*. There are many other statistical and financial reference books that also have this information.

Here are some excellent sources of business secondary research to consider:

- Periodicals and newspapers
- Trade and professional associations
- Government documents
- Company annual reports
- Patent filings
- Market research firm reports
- Directories and Annuals
- Electronic Databases
- Chambers of Commerce
- U.S. Small Business Administration
- U.S. Department of Commerce
- U.S. Government Printing Office Bookstores
- Internet and World Wide Web

You can find some of the most useful secondary research resources in a good business library. All entrepreneurs should be familiar with these resources:

- U.S. Census Bureau reports
- *U.S. Industrial Outlook*

- *Statistical Abstract of the U.S.*
- *American Demographics* magazine
- *Thomas Register of American Manufacturers*
- *Standard Rate and Data Service* (*SRDS*)
- *Encyclopedia of Associations*
- *Hoover's Handbook of American Business*
- *Sales and Marketing Management Survey of Buying Power*
- *Dun & Bradstreet* (*D&B*) *Key Business Ratios*
- *Robert Morris Associates* (*RMA*) *Annual Statement Studies*
- *Standard Industrial Classification* (*SIC*) *Manual*
- *Gale Directory of Publications and Broadcast Media*

Primary research opportunities to consider include

- Asking questions and listening at every opportunity
- Asking opinions of current and prospective customers
- Asking opinions of suppliers
- Asking opinions of family and friends
- Asking opinions of bankers, attorneys, accountants
- Personal observation of customers
- Personal observation of competitors
- Mail surveys
- Telephone surveys
- Product testing
- Focus groups (small group discussion and opinions)
- Field experiments
- Trade show display

Excellent books on developing your marketing plan and implementing specific marketing strategies are available at your library and bookstore. Look specifically for those written by Al Ries and Jack Trout, Stan Rapp and Thomas L. Collins, and Jay Conrad Levinson.

CHAPTER 5
ACTION ITEMS

Finding Your Niche and Researching Your Market

1. Segment your broad market into several submarkets.

2. Choose a target market and analyze your target customer's characteristics.

3. Develop a powerful and effective *unique selling proposition.*

CHAPTER 6

Forecasting Sales

Success in business depends on selling your product or service in sufficient quantity to justify the time and energy you put into the business. Sales are the lifeblood of every business. You could do everything else perfectly in your business, but if there are insufficient sales, you will soon be out of business.

Likewise, you could make many mistakes in other areas of the business. However, if you have a product or service that satisfies needs and you make sufficient sales, you can have a successful surviving business in spite of the mistakes. Of course, it would be even more successful without the errors, but it's the sales that make or break a business. Nothing happens until somebody sells something.

This chapter discusses the need and importance of sales forecasting. It also describes the most common techniques with examples you can adapt to your business and explain the "lifetime value of a customer" concept.

WHY ESTIMATE SALES?

Projected income and expense and cash flow are essential components of your business plan's financial analysis. They may even be a key to deciding whether or when to start your business. They are certainly important to bankers and investors who analyze your business for potential investment.

Projected expenses of a business are much easier to estimate than projected sales. Many of the resources used to estimate expenses calculate those expenses as a percentage of sales. The amount of sales is the great unknown. It is the element of the marketing and financial plan that requires the most time and the clearest and best researched analysis. If you are planning to obtain debt or equity funding for the business, you must be able to convince bankers and investors of the logic and believability of the projected sales. Spend substantial time on this section of your plan.

Most business start-up books mention the importance of a business plan and projecting sales, but they give little information on how to do it. Entrepreneurs must often fend for themselves. This chapter explains several approaches. Use or adapt the method or combination of methods that makes the most sense to your business.

The four basic steps to a proper sales forecast are

1. Determine the best method for forecasting.
2. Obtain the necessary information from secondary or primary research.
3. Perform the analysis and calculations.
4. Break down projected annual sales into months or quarters to reflect start-up, growth, and seasonality.

FORECASTING TECHNIQUES

Market potential, sales potential, and *sales forecast* have different meanings. Market potential refers to the total potential sales for a product or service over a certain geographical area for a specific time period. Sales potential refers to the total possible sales your company could make. It is a portion of the total market potential, sometimes a small portion, depending on your capacity, resources, goals, competition, and so forth. Sales forecast refers to the actual sales you predict your company will attain in the market during the time period.

There are two general methods used in forecasting sales, with many variations within the two general methods. Your first step in forecasting sales should be to determine which method, submethod, or combination of methods best suit your business.

The two types are the *market breakdown, chain-ratio*, or *top-down* method and the *market buildup* or *bottom-up* method. The market breakdown method starts at the macro level with a total population figure for the targeted market. Next, calculate several appropriate links from this top level. This further reduces the market by percentage amounts until you reach the sales forecast. This method is most appropriate for consumer goods. Practical examples and applications are explained later in the chapter.

The market buildup method starts at the micro level and tries to identify all potential buyers for a product or service. Add up the projected sales of the company for each different market to obtain the total sales forecast. This method is most appropriate for commercial and industrial sales.

Whatever analysis you use, the forecast is only as good as the data that went into it. An important part of your job as an entrepreneur is to become familiar with the sources of information available and to choose appropriately. Chapter 5 discussed market research and some major primary and secondary research resources. Visit a good business library and discuss your research needs with an experienced librarian.

There are many appropriate secondary resources available to obtain relevant sales forecast data. Specific examples include

- U.S. Census Bureau reports
- *American Demographics* magazine
- Chamber of commerce publications
- Trade and industry group publications and reports
- *Statistical Abstract of the U.S.*
- Federal, state, and local government reports
- *Sales and Marketing Management Survey of Buying Power*
- Private marketing firm reports
- *Commercial Atlas and Marketing Guide*

Possible primary research for projecting sales includes mail surveys, telephone surveys, personal questionnaires, direct observation, market tests, and focus groups. You need to determine the best choices.

Here are a few examples of how specific companies could use the market breakdown method to forecast sales. The examples also mention possible data sources. There could be many additional sources as well. These examples are for information and illustration only and will hopefully stimulate some ideas in your mind. Adapt the relevant parts to your analysis.

Company A is marketing a premium calculator to a targeted market of students. It targets the age group of twenty-five to thirty-five and plans to market only in California. Company A first determines from the U.S. Census that the potential market is 10 million. From *Sales and Marketing Management Survey of Buying Power*, Company A discovers that 12 percent of the state population is in the target age group. This reduces the market to 1,200,000. From the California Department of Education, Company A learns that 30 percent of the target age group is enrolled in college. This further reduces the market to 360,000.

Company A then conducts a survey in several classes and determines that 50 percent of the students prefer quality over price in a calculator. This further reduces the market to 180,000. Personal and telephone interviews further indicate that 30 percent plan to buy at least one calculator in the next year. Some well-accepted consumer research in a recent market research journal shows that 40 percent of those who say they are likely to purchase, actually do buy. This further reduces the market to 21,600.

Industry data and personal experience further indicate that purchasers buy an average of 1.2 calculators per year. Therefore, the total sales potential is 25,920 calculators. If the selling price is $50 per calculator, the total potential dollar sales are $1,296,000. Through market and competitor analysis, Company A believes it can obtain 25 percent of this market. Its sales forecast is $324,000 for the year. It then allocates an appropriate portion of this total annual amount to each of the twelve months.

Company B plans to open a bicycle shop near a local college. College data shows a total enrollment of 25,000, with 60 percent living on or near the campus. The remaining 40 percent are commuters. U.S. Census and local community data also show that there are 5,000 additional young professionals in the area. Company B estimates its general market of prospects to be the 15,000 noncommuting students and the 5,000 young professionals, for a total of 20,000.

Company B sets up a display booth with several bicycles on campus. Of the 1,000 people who walk by, 180 stop to look at the products and talk. The company hands out 180 questionnaires. Recipients return 136 of them. An industry trade magazine estimates that 15 percent of the general population regularly ride bicycles. Company B uses their 18 percent survey results to estimate that there are 3,600 prospects in its market.

The survey also shows that 100 of the respondents live on campus. Of this 100, 35 currently own a bike and 17 bought a bike in the last year. Company B uses the 17 percent finding to estimate that 17 percent of the 3,600 prospects, or 612, are likely to buy a new bike in the next year. Company B's analysis of the competition indicates that it should be able to sell to 25 percent of the market, meaning 153 bicycles. If the average price is $400 per bicycle, this equates to sales of $61,200.

Company C is a supermarket serving a small rural town. The town population is 20,000. The company discovers from the U.S. Census that the average local per capita income is $14,000. Company C determines from trade association data and from *Sales and Marketing Management Survey of Buying Power* that people spend 12 percent of their income on groceries. Multiplying this out, it indicates a total market potential of $33,600,000. If there are four competing supermarkets, each of similar size, Company C can expect sales of $6,720,000 on the average. Obviously, Company C hopes to do better than average. If it can show how and why, it could justify a higher sales forecast.

Company D is a local dance studio. From trade and industry data and local marketing firm research, it determines that its potential market is within a five-mile radius of the studio. Per capita income and per capita dance studio expenditures can be obtained from government and industry sources to determine the total potential sales. Analyzing the competition and Company D's niche can then help determine what portion of the total potential sales Company D can expect.

Company E is an automobile manufacturer marketing a new sports car. It has decided to use *Sales and Marketing Management's Survey of Buying Power* indices to allocate its projected sales across the country, state, and county. *Sales and Marketing Management* magazine publishes a survey of buying power for consumer markets in July and October. It also publishes a survey of buying power for industrial and commercial markets in April. The analysis uses the three factors of population, retail sales, and income to generate a buying power index for cities, counties, and metropolitan statistical areas. You can also use the data to generate your own, individually tailored and weighted, index. This personalized index should be even more accurate.

Company E assigns a relative weight to each of the three factors equaling 100 percent. It assigns demographics (age in this case) of the population as 20 percent. It assigns retail sales (economy) as 30 percent. It assigns effective buying income as 50 percent. Company E uses these weights, and the data listed for each city, county, or other market. It can then allocate its total projected sales units or revenues to the various submarkets. It could also allocate total potential market and then determine how much of that market it can reasonably attain. *Sales and Marketing Management* magazine suggests a variety of other data uses.

Here are some examples of the market buildup method:

Company F is a women's clothing store. Industry data shows that the annual sales per square foot of comparable stores average $250 to $300. Since Company F is appealing to a higher quality market, it uses $300 to multiply times the 2,000-square-foot store Company F has opened. This equates to projected total sales of $600,000. Company F reduces first-year sales by 20 percent to be more conservative and to allow for start-up and building customer awareness. Company F also obtains industry data showing the seasonality of clothing sales. It analyzes and projects the heavy and slow times into the monthly sales forecasts.

Company G is a restaurant that serves home-cooked meals for breakfast, lunch, and dinner. Its maximum serving capacity is 100 patrons. Careful analysis of its menu, the owner's experience, and industry data shows that the average "ticket" for breakfast is six dollars, for lunch is eight dollars, and for dinner is ten dollars. At each meal, customers fill an average of 50% of the seats. Each seat "turns" three times per meal. The restaurant is open six days per week. Multiplying all this out using the 312 days the restaurant is open during the year yields breakfast sales revenue of $280,800, lunch sales of $374,400, and dinner sales of $468,000. Total sales are $1,123,200.

Company G could do a more accurate projection by factoring in weekends, holidays, and beverage sales. However, this is a good example of an intelligent, well-thought-out analysis. It should impress those analyzing the plan if Company G can back up the assumptions.

Company H is an accounting business owned by Ms. H. She knows the market and the competition, and decides to bill out her services at seventy-five dollars per hour, which is lower than many accountants. Ms. H expects to work about sixty hours per week. She realizes she will use twenty hours per week for administrative and marketing activities that are not billable. Furthermore, she realizes she will likely be able to bill for 60 percent of the remaining hours. This is due to lack of client work and spending extra time that is not billable to a client.

Ms. H also plans to take two weeks of vacation after tax season and spend at least two weeks taking continuing education and computer classes. Twenty-four billable hours per week times seventy-five dollars per hour times forty-eight weeks equals $86,400 of projected revenue. Tax work is also very seasonal, so Ms. H should be sure to adjust the monthly projections to reflect this.

If your market is industrial or commercial (business to business), use a similar analysis. The starting point in gathering data, however, is often the Standard Industrial Classification (SIC) code, developed by the U.S. Bureau of the Census. Much published business information is sorted by SIC category, so it is an important business tool. The narrower you can define your market, the more specific information you can obtain to assist in your sales forecast.

Each major industrial group has a two-digit SIC code assigned. Three-digit codes further break down subgroups of industries. Four-digit codes further break down specific industries. Additional refinement even allows for six-digit and eight-digit codes. For example, code 5941 is "sporting goods and bicycle shops." Code 5941-03 is "golf, tennis, and skiing," and code 5941-0301 is "golf goods and equipment."

The ten major SIC industrial divisions are

01–09	Agriculture, forestry, fishing
10–14	Mining
15–19	Contract construction
20–39	Manufacturing
40–49	Transportation, communications, electric, gas
50–59	Wholesale and retail trade
60–67	Finance, insurance, and real estate
70–89	Services
90–93	Government
99	Others

LIFETIME VALUE OF A CUSTOMER

What is the lifetime value of an average customer to your business? It's important to know the value because it does affect your sales projections. More important, it shows how much you can afford to spend to obtain a customer. Ignoring the time value of money, you should spend whatever is necessary to obtain a new customer, as long as the cost is less than what that customer will generate in future gross profit.

You need some accurate company financial data to compute the lifetime value of a customer. First, determine the gross profit percentage (gross margin) on a typical sale. This is the sales price less the direct costs of the product or service. Next, determine the average number of purchases that an average customer makes from you in an average year. Last, determine how many years a customer typically stays with and patronizes your business. Multiply these three numbers together to determine the lifetime value of your average customer.

A local grocer determined that his gross margin was 10 percent, that the average family customer spent $300 monthly on groceries, and that the average customer stayed 5 years. The lifetime value of a customer for this business is $300 times 10 percent times 12 months per year times 5 years, or a total of $1,800. Theoretically, the grocer should be willing to spend $1,799 to obtain a new customer. You can't ignore the time value of money concept. This concept explains that a dollar today is worth more than a dollar in the future because of the ability to use and invest that dollar. The grocer would obviously not pay $1,799. However, this calculation should certainly open the grocer's eyes to spending more to obtain additional customers and to keep the current customers happy.

A package delivery service had commercial account customers who averaged sending 30 packages per week at $25 per package. That equals revenues of $18,750 per year. If there happens to be a disagreement on some service, the delivery service should keep this customer happy even if it cannot justify a refund. It should carry this philosophy down through all layers of the organization. It should impress on all its employees the lifetime value of a customer concept and empower them with the ability to obtain new customers and keep current customers by making and keeping them happy. You should do the same.

Expand the lifetime value concept even further. Getting the customer to first buy from you is the toughest sale. If you satisfy the customer, it is much easier to sell a second and third time. Additionally, you will spend less money on advertising and selling. *Reselling, upselling,* and *cross-selling* should all be considered. Reselling is selling the same item they bought before. Upselling is persuading them to buy a better, more expensive, or more sophisticated product. Cross-selling is persuading them to buy something else that's related to the original product.

Referrals can be a great source of new business. You often don't even need to persuade a referral to buy. They have been prequalified and presold by a happy customer. Factoring in referrals of new customers and their lifetime value can geometrically increase the effective lifetime value of any one customer.

To increase business profit, you need to either increase total sales revenue or decrease total business expenses. You can increase your total sales revenue in seven general ways. Review each method. Can you apply one or more to your business? Even a small improvement in each of them can produce dramatic results. Recognize that the seven methods are not mutually exclusive.

Consider these seven general techniques to increase your total sales revenue:

1. Sell the same product at the same price to more customers.
2. Sell the same product to the same customers at a higher price.
3. Persuade the customer to buy a larger quantity of the product.
4. Persuade the customer to buy other products you sell.
5. Increase the number of times a customer buys from you during the year.
6. Increase the length of time a customer continues doing business with you.
7. Obtain referrals from satisfied customers and sell products to them.

CHAPTER 6
ACTION ITEMS

Forecasting Sales

1. Use a market breakdown method to estimate your business sales. Explain the calculation.

2. Use a market buildup method to estimate your business sales. Explain the calculation.

3. Explain how you can use at least two of the seven listed general techniques to increase your sales.

CHAPTER 7

Product

Happy customers are what every business wants. If you keep your customers happy, you keep your customers. Additionally, those customers will likely buy more, and will cheerfully and loyally refer more customers.

Once you have determined your target market and customer profile, use the 4 Ps of the marketing mix to do everything possible to make the customer happy.

The 4 Ps of the marketing mix are **Product**, **Place**, **Price**, and **Promotion**. This chapter and the following five chapters discuss many of the techniques you can use to satisfy your customer. Before making any major decision with your marketing mix, ask yourself, Will this decision help me retain or increase my customers? Generally, if the answer is yes, it's a good business decision. If the answer is no, it's not a good business decision.

This chapter covers the first marketing mix variable, Product.

PRODUCT DECISIONS AND OPPORTUNITIES

The Product element includes everything that the target market values for the benefits or satisfactions it provides. *Product* includes objects, services, organizations, places, people, and ideas. It applies to both businesses selling tangible products and to businesses selling services.

Product decisions involve the following product and service decisions:

- Physical product
- Sight, sound, smell, feel, taste
- Services provided
- Features and benefits
- Accessories and options
- Functions and uses
- Guarantees and warranties
- Quality
- Style and image projected
- Sizes
- Installation
- Instructions
- Packaging
- Brand names
- Product lines
- Delivery
- Return policies
- Environmental impact
- Regulatory issues
- Potential legal liability

Give careful thought to each possible product decision. Make your business the best it can be, and keep your customers happy.

One way to view product and service opportunities is to classify them as *present* or *new*, and to also classify markets as *present* or *new*. The matrix and the four possible opportunities that result look like this:

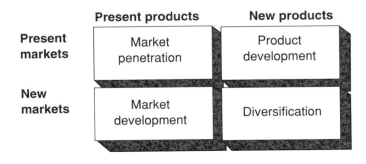

There can be many variations and subparts of these four general ways of viewing product and market opportunities. However, these four basic concepts should open your mind to untapped potential. You can increase sales and profits in many different ways.

Market penetration allows you to increase sales of your present product in your present market. Persuade current customers to use more by promoting new uses or by finding and satisfying more customers within your present market.

Market development allows you to take your present product to a new market. This could be a new demographic market within your current geographic area. It could also be a totally new geographic market, such as a new city, state, or country. It could even involve a new use of the product that opens up a whole new market.

Product development allows you to keep satisfying your current happy customers who already trust you. Think of new and related products that you could sell to this same market. What items would be a natural match? Consider partnering with other companies or doing cross-referrals if you don't want to handle total product development yourself. Loyal customers are a very valuable asset. You have a head start on new product sales if your current customers are happy with you and with your present product or service.

Try **diversification** last, if you try it at all. Taking a present product to a new market or developing a new product for a present market is more often successful. Diversification has weakened or destroyed many companies who forgot what made them successful in the first place. Even very large national and multinational firms have had problems when they try to diversify too much. Smaller businesses should learn a valuable lesson. Diversification is good in investments, but often very bad in business. Be careful.

If you are thinking of taking a new tangible product to a present or new market, a yes answer to the following questions is highly recommended:

1. Is the technology simplified?
2. Is the product obviously unique?
3. Is the benefit obvious to and desired by potential customers?
4. Is the market open?
5. Are your customers easy to target?

6. Can you realistically sell the product for three to five times its direct cost?
7. Can you effectively package the product?
8. Can you afford to make your models, prototypes, and initial production runs?
9. Can you find a contract manufacturer willing to absorb some of the start-up manufacturing costs?
10. Can you find market insiders to help you?
11. Is the product easy to distribute, and does a cost-effective distribution network exist?
12. Is the market size of the distribution network large enough to justify your time and expense?

FEATURES AND BENEFITS AND PRODUCT COMPONENTS

Customers buy only products and services that have perceived benefits greater than perceived cost. You must clearly express and fully explain all the benefits to the customer.

People often confuse features and benefits. Features are elements of the product or service that deliver a benefit. Customers buy the benefits, not the features. However, business owners and salespeople often forget or ignore this. They spend their time concentrating on the features. Features are often technical, and the customer does not easily understand them. Benefits should be very clear.

Here are a few examples to illustrate the difference:

FEATURE	BENEFIT
Airbags	Fewer and less severe injuries
Large type	Ease of reading
Digital recording	Hiss-free listening
Soft leather shoes	Comfortable walking
Mercedes logo	Increased self-esteem and status

Identify the most basic need of the customer. It is that one need that is the most powerful and effective at a deep level. It is the real reason why the customer buys. If you can appeal to one or two basic needs and clearly satisfy them, your business will be very successful.

Here are the most basic reasons why people buy. See how many apply to your business. Accent the most powerful ones. Clearly drive home the point in all your marketing by concentrating on one or more of these motivations:

- To make money
- To save money
- To save time
- To avoid effort
- To achieve comfort
- To enjoy good health
- To protect family and friends
- To be in style
- To own beautiful things
- To satisfy appetites
- To stimulate others
- To be safe
- To be happy
- To have fun
- To escape pain
- To be praised
- To be popular
- To attract the opposite sex
- To conserve possessions
- To satisfy curiosity
- To avoid criticism
- To realize individuality
- To take advantage of opportunities
- To avoid trouble
- To protect their reputation
- To conserve memories

Assess the needs of your target market and the benefits of your product or service. Review Abraham Maslow's famous Hierarchy of Needs analysis on page 94. Maslow divided human needs into five categories. His analysis shows that humans must first substantially satisfy the lowest level of needs. They can then move on and strive to meet higher-level needs.

Physiological needs, such as hunger and thirst are at the bottom level. Safety needs such as security and protection are next. Social needs, such as love and a sense of belonging, are at the third level. Above this level are the higher-level needs that many never attain. Esteem needs, which include self-esteem, recognition, and status, are at the fourth level. Self-actualization needs, such as self-realization and self-development, are at the top level.

Understand your product and where it fits in the hierarchy for different types of customers. It may be at different levels for different markets. Use psychology to show and tell how your product or service can satisfy some of these needs.

Maslow's Hierarchy of Needs

Carefully analyze all the components of your business or product. You might spot great opportunities to differentiate yourself from the competition. A series of concentric circles or rings, each of which represents specific activities or tangible attributes, best illustrates the concept.

The Components of a Product

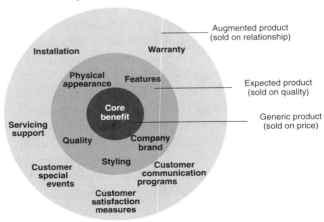

The **generic product**, or core product, is the basic product or service sold with nothing added. For a retail men's clothing store, it is the availability for sale of basic white shirts and dark blue slacks. Few can stay in business selling pure generic products. Price alone sells pure generic products.

The **expected product** includes the generic product plus sufficient attributes and activities to meet a customer's minimal expectations. For the clothing store, these would likely include good quality and various styles, colors, and sizes. It would also likely include brand names, reasonable prices, professional service, and credit card acceptance. Quality, rather than price, is generally more important when selling expected products.

The **augmented product** goes beyond merely offering what the customer expects. The goal is to offer customers more than what they think they need or have become accustomed to expect. The clothing store could offer in-store, one-hour tailoring; personal shoppers; and computerized fittings. It could host special events, serve complimentary gourmet coffee, offer home delivery, and feature an unlimited return policy. These and many other activities and attributes are being used in the business world by some of the best and most successful companies. The relationship with the customer, rather than price or quality, is generally most important when selling augmented products.

The **potential product** is everything potentially feasible to attract and retain customers. The augmented product consists of everything possible that has been or is being done, while the potential product refers to what is possible, but not yet attempted or attained. It is the charting of new and unknown, but exciting, territory. Someone has to be the first. Why shouldn't it be you? Keep on top of changing products, markets, and conditions. Use your imagination and insight. Experiment and have fun.

NAMES, LOGOS, COLORS, AND PACKAGES

Entrepreneurs don't always see the importance and value of good business and product names. Names do not often seem important early on, as more pressing needs of the business are being met. Nevertheless, it is wise to spend sufficient time choosing an appropriate business or product name. It will pay dividends in the future. Many of the well-known companies today could lose all their physical and monetary assets and would retain substantial value with their name alone.

Think down the road many years. A powerful and protected business or product name can give your business added value that can continue beyond your career. If a sale or inheritance of the business occurs, a powerful name will add value.

The naming process can be fun but also frustrating. The best names combine the marketing benefits of a *descriptive* name and the legal benefits of a *coined* or *arbitrary* name. Try to attain the best of both worlds with a *suggestive* name.

The four basic tests for assessing the power of a name are

1. **Distinctiveness**. The name should immediately distinguish the business from its competitors. Stay away from traditional or generic names such as first, national, American, and united. Break away from the crowd.

2. **Relevance**. The name should convey the nature or benefit of the service to identify and position your company in the customer's mind.

3. **Memorability**. Be able to understand, use, and recall the name easily. Stress brevity, simplicity, ease of pronunciation, and ease of spelling.

4. **Flexibility**. The name should accommodate the inevitable changes in the organization, economy, products, and strategies. Be careful of geographic and product or service limitations.

Here are some more guidelines in choosing a good name:

- Pick a name that reflects your identity.
- Your name should have a positive ring. Avoid negatives. Your name should make people enthusiastic and optimistic.
- Don't become caught up in trends or fads. Be focused on the long term.
- Pick a name that looks and sounds attractive.
- Consider a name that starts with A if you plan to advertise in the Yellow Pages.
- Avoid puns and jokes. Customers want benefits, not humor. Remember that you will live with the name for a long time.
- Be careful of technology-sensitive names that could require changes in the future.

- Generally avoid names that include the name of you or any other person. Your name is not a benefit to a customer.
- Pick a name that invites and persuades customers to buy your product.
- Pick a name that can be a headline by itself.
- Pick a name that appeals to your target market's emotions.
- Don't overpromise and underperform. Live up to your name.
- Be sure to obtain proper legal protection for your name.
- Research the meaning and sound of names in foreign languages and cultures.

A good logo helps position your company, giving your business an image and an easy-to-remember hook in the mind of the prospect. Today you have only a few seconds to capture a customer's attention. A logo can make the crucial difference. One study showed that 55 percent of consumers react differently to a company's logo along with the name, than to the name alone. The reaction to the logo and name combination is generally more positive.

If possible, use one graphic icon that relates to the business as your specific logo. Give some thought to an appropriate representation of the quality, creativity, and other traits of your business. Apple Computer's logo is a great example. It's simple, creative, universal, and memorable.

If you cannot utilize a relevant graphic icon to represent the business, use a simple general icon or symbol. Consider even using just the name in an attractive logo format. The blue lined letters of the IBM logo and the swoosh of the Nike logo are good examples of such general quality logos.

When using a logo, be sure to always add the name of the business under the logo. You want to insure that people not only recognize the logo, but associate it with your business. Don't use a cheap, common, or difficult-to-understand logo. Hire a graphic designer if necessary. Be sure to acquire all legal rights for present and future use from the designer.

Colors and shapes have meanings and feelings attached to them. Research the visibility, retention, preference, and association traits of different colors and shapes. Recognize that colors often have substantially different significance and meaning in certain countries and cultures.

Research data is available on color and shape psychology. Know your target market and the qualities of your business that you want to emphasize. This allows you to choose appropriate colors and shapes for your logo, letterhead, business cards, signs, packaging, uniforms, and products.

Packaging is very important for many products. Here are a few ideas on designing your package:

- List enough information on the package for the consumer to make an educated buying decision.
- Inspire confidence with a consistent quality of design, colors, and materials.
- Consider a window to show what's inside.
- Stay within the standard industry size guidelines.
- Compare your package with the competition. Would a consumer pick yours?
- Make the package competitive in shape, size, color, labeling and appearance.
- Use consistent and easy-to-read names, symbols, themes, and typeface.
- Use the package as a marketing tool that encourages and suggests new uses.
- Try to have your product placed in a dominant, eye-level position in the store.
- Continually test the package design. Solicit retailer and consumer opinions to improve it.

CHAPTER 7
ACTION ITEMS

Product

1. Complete a features and benefits analysis for your product or service.

2. List as many possible "potential product" elements for your product or service as you can envision.

3. Develop a name and logo for your business. What does it signify?

CHAPTER 8

Place

Customers want your product or service today. How do you get it to the consumer in a cost-effective, efficient, and acceptable manner? These are the concerns you have in satisfying the *place* decisions of the marketing mix.

Location of your business may be a key decision. Chapter 15 discusses location in great detail. Use your own industry research, ideas, and analysis for other *place* decisions such as transporting, handling, storing, displaying, and processing. This chapter concentrates on describing the many distribution possibilities for products and services.

Many businesses are successful, not because they have a unique product or service, but because they have a unique or effective way of distributing products or services. Companies such as WalMart, Home Shopping Network, Land's End, and Amway are examples of successful businesses built on a distribution system rather than a product. If you have a better or less expensive way to deliver products to consumers, you don't need a unique product. If you have ideas for distributing the products to new markets, such as exporting, importing, or selling to the government, you don't need a unique product. Make your money selling and distributing others' products.

Don't limit yourself to the traditional ways of selling your product. Keep an open mind as you review the many possible ways of selling and distributing. Try one or two new methods. They could dramatically increase your success.

SELLING CHANNELS

This section discusses five general categories of product and service marketing and distribution. The section explains specific methods within each category. The five major categories are

1. Market directly to the consumer
2. Market through the government
3. Market through distribution channels
4. Market through foreign trade
5. Market through specialty channels

Market Directly to the Consumer

There are many ways to market directly to the consumer. One traditional method is **door-to-door** sales. Vacuum cleaners, housewares, cosmetics, and encyclopedias are some of the products successfully marketed door-to-door directly to the consumer. Some firms sell other products similarly to businesses. This method works particularly well if your product needs demonstration.

Party plan selling is similar. Companies selling cookware, cosmetics, clothing, and jewelry use this method successfully. A sponsor invites a group of people to a home party for a demonstration of the product. The sponsor uses premiums, gifts, and various sales incentives in an informal and fun atmosphere.

Direct mail is often a great way to sell your product. If you know the demographics and other traits of your ideal customer, you can use a rifle-shot approach, rather than a shotgun approach, to deliver the message to your potential market. The key to successful direct mail is to have a good product, a good offer, and a good mailing list. All of these require careful analysis.

Send your own mailings to lists of potential businesses or consumers. Review the wealth of information in *Standard Rate and Data Service* (*SRDS*) publications. Contact a mailing list broker to discuss possibilities. Consider advertising in relevant magazines and journals that your target market reads. Add your product to an existing product catalog. Add your product information to mailings sent by noncompeting and compatible companies.

Use **telemarketing** to reach customers directly by telephone. Many products sold this way have bad reputations. However, there is no doubt that professional and appropriate telemarketing is very effective.

Multilevel or network marketing is a popular distribution method with many products. A network of friends, relatives, and coworkers, with various layers of commission payouts, market the product. Multilevel marketing is popular in recessionary periods, is not capital intensive, and gives people major incentives to build an independent business. However, this is a highly regulated industry. It has high attrition rates among salespeople, and it requires constant effort to keep salespeople motivated.

Television infomercials are often expensive to produce and run, but for the right product, they can result in huge sales. There are heavy up-front costs, but television can reach a large number of people at one time and can produce fast results. Infomercials are excellent for product demonstrations, but the product must have a high markup to be a viable candidate. Be sure to use reputable experts in this field.

Home shopping networks can be a great source for the right products. Your profit margin is often quite small, but you hope to make it up in quantity.

Pay-per-call 900 phone number lines do not have the best reputation, but they may be an appropriate revenue-generator or service add-on for your product or service. You can provide entertainment or give out information with the lines. Date lines, talk lines, sports lines, and adult lines are all popular uses. Direct response and transactional applications can also utilize pay-per-call. Examples include promotions, sweepstakes, polling, surveying, fundraising, sampling, customer service, order entry, and fax-back. The real advantage is that they allow the marketer to share the cost of a service with the customers who benefit. Local numbers, toll numbers, toll-free numbers, and pay-per-call numbers all have a place in business. Consider those that best meet your company's needs.

Computer databases and the **Internet,** accessed through modems, will continue to grow and expand in the upcoming years. Many will make and lose fortunes in this field. Use it wisely. The Internet is a powerful tool to market products and services through Home Pages on the World Wide Web. It is cost-effective and far reaching. You can efficiently reach international markets and rural markets. Access is available seven days per week, twenty-four hours per day.

Market Through the Government

The **federal**, **state**, and **local governments** all buy many products and services. Why shouldn't you participate? Determine how to bid on projects and whether you qualify for any special considerations, such as minority-owned, or women-owned businesses. Just being a small business qualifies you for certain set-asides.

Check your local daily and business newspapers for notices from local, state, and federal agencies with specifications about what they want to buy. Review special publications like *Commerce Business Daily*. The U.S. Commerce Department publishes it weekdays. It lists many opportunities and news related to upcoming projects.

Join government agency mailing lists that seem appropriate to your business. Review the SBA's *U.S. Government Purchasing and Sales Directory*. Write to the specific agency that interests you and request that your name be added to their mailing list. If you see a solicitation that interests you, write for more details. Consider applying for Small Business Innovation Research (SBIR) grants. Chapter 13 describes them in detail. Keep your eyes and ears open for opportunities. Consider using a consultant or specialist to assist you in writing proposals for contracts or grants. Experience in this field is helpful.

Market Through Distribution Channels

Department stores may be an excellent source for selling your product if you can place it in the store. Determine what department within the store your product best fits, and talk with the buyer for that department. Listen and learn from buyers. They have a wealth of information. Consider contacting a *resident buyer* who represents many department stores across the state or the country. This is more effective and efficient than trying to contact all stores directly.

You may want to sell through chain stores, discount stores, supermarkets, leased departments, and dealers. You can try to contact all these channels directly, or you can use sales representatives, wholesalers, or jobbers.

Independent sales representatives are often the most appropriate choice for small business. The sales representative works on commission. The representative does not take title, but is merely an order taker. You pay the commission after the sales representative completes the sale. Find some good representatives who know your industry. Carefully negotiate compensation, payment, territory, competing products, and other necessary terms. Draft a clear, concise written agreement. Consider using different representatives for different markets. Require regular reports and keep the representative updated with current information, sales literature, and products. Keep close watch on performance, and don't hesitate to change.

The easiest way to find a sales agent is through the annual directory published by the Manufacturers' Agents National Association (MANA). Contact them at P.O. Box 3467, Laguna Hills, CA 92654; (714) 859-4040. MANA is the trade association for distribution firms and manufacturers' agents. MANA publishes a monthly magazine called *Agency Sales*, a huge selection of research reports, and a series of special reports.

Wholesalers and **jobbers** differ from sales representatives in that they own and warehouse your product. They are able to do this by buying your product cheaper than the retailer buys it from you. They then resell to the independent dealer at the regular dealer price. You have less profit selling to a wholesaler, but also less risk. Often sales representatives and wholesalers are both involved in the distribution chain. Typically, a manufacturer sells through a sales rep. A sales rep calls on the wholesaler. The wholesaler buys from the manufacturer and resells it to a retailer. The retailer then sells it to the consumer.

Chain stores, which are common in drug stores, variety stores, and auto supply stores, can be a tremendous source of sales. You usually sell to only one buyer, and the product goes in all the stores. Chain stores know their power and may ask for concessions. Be wary about giving any long-range exclusives or selling on consignment. You want to be able to sell elsewhere, and you don't want the products coming back.

Discount stores can be another great source of sales. However, because it is their policy to sell products below normal retail, you run the risk of hurting your regular accounts that sell at a higher price. Consider disguising your product for the discount store by using a private label and changing the name, packaging, and color.

Consider **supermarkets** even if you are not selling a food product. Supermarkets sell housewares, stationery, magazines, toys, and more. They offer tremendous visibility.

Many specialty stores and discount stores **lease** out certain **departments**. Outside parties often lease photography, optometry, jewelry, pharmaceutical, and fast food sections of stores. The organizations leasing these departments may have such sections in many stores. One buyer can help get you in multiple locations.

Send direct mail to distributors as well as final consumers. Consider supplementing your normal distribution methods with appropriate and regular mailings to wholesalers and retailers.

Market Through Foreign Trade

Exporting and **importing** open up vast new markets. These may not be the first new markets you venture into after starting a business. However, certainly consider them down the road after you have proved the viability and success of your product.

The federal government greatly encourages exporting your product to other countries. The U.S. Commerce Department is the agency to contact. They have a wealth of information on countries, products, regulations, and resources. They often present seminars on relevant international business topics.

Importing products from other countries to sell in the United States can be quite profitable. Importing materials to implement in your product can also be profitable. U.S. Customs is the federal agency to contact regarding all the rules.

If you do become involved with international trade, take advantage of all the government and private resources available to assist you. Locate your closest World Trade Center to see what they offer. Check the local colleges and universities for classes, seminars, and counseling.

Market Through Specialty Channels

Market your product or service through numerous other channels. Here are a few ideas on these *specialty* channels.

Armed forces post exchanges carry an assortment of merchandise equal to that of many department stores. Contact them directly, or obtain a list of the exchanges from the U.S. Defense Department.

Premiums are those items given away by companies in exchange for the consumer doing something or buying something in return. Could companies use your product as an incentive premium? This is a multibillion-dollar industry.

Advertising specialties are the giveaway items with a company advertising message printed on it. Pens, coffee cups, caps, key rings, memo pads, calendars, and executive gifts are all common examples. Would your product be a suitable novelty, gift, or souvenir for a company?

Selling **franchises** and **business opportunities**, or **licensing** your product, service, or idea, are more sophisticated ways of marketing and distributing. They can greatly expand your market reach if used properly. Be sure to obtain specialized market and legal advice before venturing into these areas.

Trade shows, fairs, and **expositions** can all be important distribution methods and excellent ways to learn more about your market. Representatives from everywhere attend industry trade shows. This could be a good opportunity to meet and interview potential agents, talk with decision makers, and even learn from the competition. Plan and organize your time well. Follow up after the show with the contacts you made.

DISTRIBUTION EXPECTATIONS

Manufacturers, wholesalers, and retailers all have different needs and expectations. Conflict can occur if they don't meet these needs and expectations. Here are some typical expectations that each has about the other two:

Manufacturer expects the Wholesaler

- To be familiar with the manufacturer's products
- Not to carry competitor's brands
- To pass along customer ideas and complaints
- To sell at competitive margins
- To pass along discounts
- To pay on time
- To actively push the manufacturer's products
- To allow credit for retailers
- To service many retailers
- To meet shipping schedules
- To keep adequate inventories

Manufacturer expects the Retailer

- To be familiar with the manufacturer's products
- To honor warranties
- To provide adequate display space
- To pass along customer ideas and complaints
- Not to develop private brands
- To offer such services as delivery and installation
- To maintain low prices
- To pass along discounts
- To run advertisements on manufacturer's products
- To keep a quality image
- To service many customers
- To keep adequate stock
- To maintain convenient hours
- To open branch stores and to deliver

Wholesaler expects the Manufacturer

- To produce quality products
- To provide packaging
- To provide a wide, deep line to satisfy customers
- Not to sell directly to retailers
- To sell at low prices and give price concessions
- To provide moneys for extensive consumer advertising
- To offer liberal credit terms
- To give exclusive distribution rights

Wholesaler expects the Retailer

- To accept wholesaler's assortment
- To provide adequate display space
- To maintain low prices
- To pass along discounts
- To pay promptly
- To promote wholesaler's lines
- To order on a regular basis
- To place orders in bulk quantities

Retailer expects the Manufacturer

- To produce quality products
- To provide a wide, deep line to satisfy customers
- To introduce new products

- To honor manufacturer's warranties
- To provide attractive packaging
- To suggest retail prices which permit large margins
- To provide in-store displays and give advice
- To provide moneys for extensive customer advertising
- To supply adequate amounts of popular items
- To deliver shipments on time

Retailer expects the Wholesaler

- To provide a wide assortment
- To know the product line
- To provide low prices and allow price concessions
- To have helpful, nonaggressive salespersons
- To provide cooperative advertising
- To allow liberal credit
- To provide fast delivery in small quantities
- To offer a liberal return policy

RETAIL SALES OPPORTUNITIES

Retail sales have evolved into a complex array of different, but sometimes overlapping, store types. Here is a list of various retail store types to consider in your marketing:

Department stores buy merchandise at a discount, take a full markup, and offer a full range of shopper services. These include credit accounts, private shopping assistance, in-store restaurant, special orders, deliveries, and refunds. Examples are Nordstrom, Macy's, and Saks Fifth Avenue.

Discounters buy at a discount, sell at lower markup than department stores, and do not offer shopper services. Examples are K-Mart, WalMart, and Target.

Moderate-price stores buy lower-priced goods at a discount, take standard retail markup, and may offer some shopper services. Examples are Mervyns and Miller's Outpost.

Power retailers buy in huge quantities, push vendors for big volume discounts, and sell merchandise at small markup to keep prices low. Examples are Home Depot, Circuit City, and J.C. Penney.

Warehouse retailers buy in huge quantities from manufacturers that give these stores the best deal. Warehousers take minimal markup. They package merchandise to move rapidly in large volume. They offer no shopper services. Examples are PriceCostco, Pace, and Sam's Club.

Off-pricers buy from manufacturers or vendors at the best discount available. They usually carry the same merchandise type as department stores, but the styles and colors may be past fashion prime, and labels vary. They take a smaller markup and offer no special services. Examples are Ross stores and Marshalls.

Clearance or closeout stores buy excess unsold inventory from manufacturers or from other retailers. Full service department stores may operate them to dispose of unsold merchandise. Examples are Pic 'n' Save, Nordstrom Rack, and Filene's basement.

Factory outlets carry surplus production, returns, discontinued merchandise, and goods produced to meet orders later canceled. Manufacturers often operate them.

What are the sources for off-price and clearance stores?

Manufacturer overruns. Manufacturers often overestimate the demand for a product and produce too much. They sell the leftovers at low prices.

Factory downtime. Many manufacturers have slow periods when it is cheaper to continue running the assembly line than to close it. At these times, they often agree to produce products at a fraction of normal costs.

Warehouse relocations and closures. Manufacturers and wholesalers regularly relocate or close warehouses, creating the need to sell large amounts of merchandise.

Canceled orders. A retailer or wholesaler may go out of business or cancel an order before delivery.

Discontinued products. Manufacturers introduce thousands of new products a year to replace older lines. They also test-market and then discontinue many new products. Other leftovers include out-of-style designs or colors, or fad items past their peak.

Buy backs. The manufacturer sells the merchandise to a retailer. The manufacturer guarantees the sale within a specified time period. At the end of the period, the manufacturer buys back the remainder, then sells it at a substantial discount.

Customs appropriations. U.S. Customs often appropriates and auctions abandoned or confiscated products.

CHAPTER 8
ACTION ITEMS

Place

1. Determine at least two ways to effectively market directly to your final consumer.

2. Determine at least two effective distribution channels to market through.

3. Determine at least two retail sales opportunities you can effectively use.

CHAPTER 9

Price

Great quality, impeccable service, and a low price — that's what customers want. You would like to give them all three, but it's not economically viable. The best business owners know that, and they concentrate on giving the customer two of the three. The whole marketing focus of the company stresses specifics of the two general traits. They either ignore or minimize the third trait. Often they carefully explain why and how they chose the company philosophy. They highlight benefits.

Pricing your product or service is important whether or not you use price as one of your company benefits. Entrepreneurs often give very little thought to price decisions. However, an appropriate pricing strategy can increase sales, increase profits, and separate your business from the competition. Creative pricing also adds fun and new opportunities to your business.

This chapter discusses the basic pricing strategies used by most businesses. It explains the mathematics of pricing. It also suggests some new ideas to stimulate your creativity, allowing you to break away from the crowd in pricing decisions.

Be sensitive to the psychology of pricing and the explanation of the price to customers. You may want to delete *price* and *cost* from your vocabulary, and instead use the term *investment*. Instead of *buying*, use *owning*. Talk about your product or service being *more economical* rather than *cheaper*. Break down the *investment* into a daily, weekly, or yearly amount to illustrate how it really makes sense. Above all, stress the benefits, long term and short term, tangible and intangible, that the customer will derive from the transaction.

BASIC PRICING STRATEGIES

Pricing strategy starts with the premise that there is a *floor* and a *ceiling* for establishing a price. The floor, the amount that you cannot price below, is your cost. This is certainly true in theory and over the long term. However, cost is a complex concept. Obviously it includes the direct cost of the product or service you are selling. However, if you want to guarantee profit to the business, you also need to include indirect costs such as overhead.

There are times in a business when you do sell below cost, however you define cost. Perhaps you have old or perishable stock you need to sell now. It is better to obtain something for it and send it out the door. Penetration pricing strategies and *loss leaders* may also necessitate selling below cost. However, for most purposes, treat cost as the floor for pricing. Obtain solid data on your costs so that you know exactly what they are and what price you need to charge to cover them.

The *ceiling*, over which you cannot price, is not an exact amount. The demand for the product and its competition determine the ceiling. Another good reason to differentiate your product from the competition, at least in the mind of the customer, is to allow you more height to the ceiling. You need market, customer, and competitor research to determine how high you can reasonably price your product or service.

Most businesses use one of three basic pricing strategies. There are many variations within these three strategies. This section discusses a few. A later section on creative pricing strategies discusses many more.

Cost plus is the simplest pricing strategy. You set your prices by determining your costs and adding a standard markup to the costs. In setting the markup percentage, it is very important to consider all your costs, direct and indirect. These must all be covered to insure a profit, allowing you to continue in business. After determining the markup, apply it to the direct cost of the product to determine price.

Cost plus applies to products or services. It is easy to calculate, once you have determined the markup percentage. It insures coverage of costs. Cost plus is an appropriate method when the total cost of a project is difficult to estimate. Construction, research, and government projects are good candidates for cost plus pricing. However, the cost plus strategy fails to relate the price or quality of service to customer needs. It also fails to reflect the different price sensitivities of different markets, and it doesn't encourage cost reduction or control.

Competitive pricing is a strategy where you determine the price of the major competitor(s), and you price the same or slightly under them. You may be able to add charges for extras like fast service or long-term guarantees, if the market wants these and is willing to pay more.

Competitive pricing is fairly simple and an easy method to start with. It provides some competitive advantage in the short run, but it doesn't allow you to separate yourself from the competition. It may also result in price wars, with a competitor always claiming a lower price, and doesn't guarantee that you will cover all costs. It also does not necessarily reflect value to the customer. It's a "me-too" philosophy that often continues without any thought.

Value-in-use pricing takes more research but is often worth it in the long run. Value-in-use pricing defines the value of the product or service in terms of what the consumer would lose, or what the consumer would have to pay, if the product or service was not available. Apply value-in-use to a powerful computer program that saves the customer from having to hire another employee. Apply it to a home or car security system that safeguards a priceless asset.

You have tremendous leeway in increasing the price of your product or service if you can clearly explain the tangible and intangible benefits to customers. Place a dollar value on the benefits. This strategy requires market research to measure value, and it may not be competitive in a price-sensitive market.

Your final pricing decision will likely be a combination of these three basic methods and perhaps several more. The important point is to make an informed, intelligent decision on price that is consistent with your whole business concept and strategy. Consider testing different prices to determine the best choice. Understand the economic concept of supply and demand. Make a pricing decision that makes the most sense to your bottom line. Make a rational, informed decision.

MATHEMATICS OF PRICING

The mathematics of pricing is not complex, but the entrepreneur needs to fully understand it. This section discusses the three concepts of determining cost, establishing a markup, and setting prices in a distribution channel.

Determine the total cost of your product or service to set the theoretical *floor* for your pricing decisions and to guarantee that you start and run a profitable business. If you don't know what your costs are, decisions are guesswork.

Cost accounting is a detailed and complex subject that accounting students explore as an upper-division subject. This section discusses only the general components. A complete and professional analysis may require you to hire a trained cost accountant.

Material, labor, and overhead constitute the total cost of producing a product or service.

Materials cost is the cost of materials used directly in the final product. For a retail store, it is the purchase cost of the product itself. For a service business, it may be nothing, or a nominal amount, for items like paper.

Labor cost is the cost of work directly applied to making or selling the product or service. Compute the cost of labor per hour. Be sure to include the taxes and fringe benefits paid to the direct labor. A reasonable add-on for taxes and fringe benefits is often 20 percent to 30 percent. Carefully analyze your specific costs. Health insurance, pensions, and workers' compensation are a few benefits that can drastically alter this add-on amount.

Overhead cost includes all costs other than direct materials and direct labor. Overhead is all indirect cost that relates to the product or service. These include support personnel, insurance, taxes, depreciation, rent, accounting, advertising, utilities, and supplies.

You should determine an appropriate relationship between direct material or direct labor cost and the utilization of the overhead. Once you establish this relationship, apply an overhead rate to fairly allocate the overhead cost to the products or services. You may need professional assistance to calculate this accurately and to periodically update it.

Markup and *margin* are terms frequently used in business. However, many misunderstand or misuse the terms. Markup and margin are exactly the same when expressing the concepts in dollars. Both concepts represent the difference between the cost of the product and the selling price.

If you express margin as a percentage, you always figure it on the selling price. If you express markup as a percentage, you can figure it as a percentage of cost or of selling price. For example, if an item costs you $1.20, and you sell it for $1.60, the margin and markup are $.40 in dollar terms. The margin as a percentage as well as the markup on selling price is 25 percent ($.40/$1.60). The markup on cost is 33¹/₃ percent ($.40/$1.20).

Margin, or markup on sale, is the better method to guarantee profitability. Markup on cost is an easier calculation to establish a selling price. Whichever method you use, ensure that the original analysis you used in setting a rate covers all the costs plus a reasonable profit. Conversion tables are available that make it easy to convert markup on cost to markup on selling price, and markup on selling price to markup on cost, if necessary.

Consider using a standard markup on most or all products for ease of use. Consider using variable markups if there are substantial cost differences, such as advertising, in selling different products.

If you are selling your product or service through a distribution channel, structure your pricing so that everyone in the channel attains their expected or desired profit. Work backward from the final price charged to the end user. Perform the appropriate calculations for each distribution channel. Give careful thought to the effect on the consumer and on the distribution channel members. Some of them may be in competition.

For example, assume you are a manufacturer who sells to a distributor, who sells to a retailer, who then sells to a final consumer. The expected retail price to the consumer is $1,000; the retailer needs a 50 percent margin (markup on selling price), and the distributor needs a 30 percent margin.

Working backward, the retailer would need to buy the item from the distributor for $500. The distributor would need to buy the item from the manufacturer for $350. You need to realize this.

You need to insure that costs will allow you to sell the item for $350 and still make a fair profit. You also need to consider this pricing effect on any other distribution methods you use.

CREATIVE PRICING TECHNIQUES

Open your mind to some more creative pricing opportunities. Only one or two of these choices could be the key to making your business unique. Take a chance. Test some of the methods. Use them on special occasions. Have fun. Be the first in your industry to adapt one of these strategies to your business.

Some of these strategies are variations of the basic pricing methods previously discussed. Some are new strategies that could be the foundation for your whole business pricing decision. Many are extras you can add or use on special occasions to help stimulate interest. Use your imagination and see how many you can apply to your business.

Skimming pricing. Set initial prices relatively high to recover the initial capital spent developing the product or opening a store. Feature quality, service, or uniqueness. Competition will often force lower prices. Use skimming if you are one of the first out with new technology or are capitalizing on a current trend or fad.

Penetration pricing. Set initial prices low at first to quickly penetrate the market. As business develops, gradually raise prices to a more profitable level. Feature low prices and convenience. This is a good pricing technique for generating immediate cash flow. Don't set the price so low that customers believe your product or service is inferior.

Promotional pricing. Set special low prices to introduce new products or lines. Consider two-for-one specials, end-of-season sales. Utilize this method to maintain traffic, stimulate demand, or make room for new merchandise.

Loss-leader pricing. Select one item, and advertise it at below cost to create store traffic and sell other regularly priced items. Make sure you have the items in stock and plan to sell them without trying to illegally switch customers to higher-priced items. Loss-leader pricing is appropriate for items that already have low margins, but can drive sales of accessories or related items.

Prestige and image pricing. This is nonprice competition. The business offers the finest merchandise, the best service, free delivery, or friendly, knowledgeable clerks in plush, convenient surroundings. Ads may not even mention price.

Bundling or unbundling pricing. Sell products or services together as packages, or break them apart and price them separately. Season tickets, stereo equipment, and automobiles are sold using this strategy. Stress the value and benefits.

Time-period pricing. This technique is also called seasonal discount pricing. Products and services have seasons. Some are fairly short, such as ripe bananas, and some are longer, such as the tax season for accountants. Consider pricing your products or services to adjust for obsolete or perishable products and variations in supply and demand. Examples are bargain summer rental rates in Palm Springs and lower fees for accounting work during nontax season. Early-bird dinner specials and higher ticket prices for movies during weekends and evenings are other examples. Time-period pricing can both smooth and increase cash flow.

Trial pricing. Make it easy by lowering the risk for a customer to try out what you sell. Special health club starter memberships and free hours of online computer access are examples. Trial pricing is beneficial for new products or services that have not been fully accepted.

Value-added pricing. Include free or low-cost value-added services, without raising the price, to appeal to bargain shoppers. Special reports to accompany a magazine subscription and hotel airport pickups are examples.

Pay-one-price pricing. Provide unlimited use of a service or product at one set price. All-you-can-eat buffets, super passes at amusement parks, and copier service contracts are examples.

Performance pricing. Performance, or value received, determines the amount customers pay. Contingent fees to lawyers, investment managers' compensation tied to performance, and games of chance or skill are examples. This reduces the risk to the customer.

Payment plan pricing. Rather than adjust the total price, adjust the payments to make your price seem different and more economical. Use four payments of $9.99 rather than $40. Explain that a $10,000 investment that will last ten years really only costs $1,000 per year, $20 per week, or $2.75 per day.

Shifting costs pricing. Pass on certain costs directly to your customer, and do not include them in your price. Lawyers charging for phone calls, photocopies, and travel in addition to fees, and hotels charging for phone calls, movies, and food or refreshments in the room are examples.

Creative variable pricing. Set up a "price per" pricing schedule tied to a related variable. Lunch pricing per pound, children's haircuts priced per inch of height, and marina space billed per boat foot are examples.

Different name or segment pricing. Sell essentially the same product, under different names, to appeal to different markets or different distribution channels. Clothing and electronics equipment are examples.

Captive pricing. Lock in your customer by selling the system cheap, and then profit by selling high-margin consumables. Selling razors at cost with all the profit in the blades is one example. Selling copiers slightly above cost with all the profit in the paper and toner cartridges is another. Giving away cellular telephones with all the profit in the monthly fees is a third example.

Product-line pricing. Establish a range of price points within your line. Structure the prices to encourage customers to buy your highest-profit product or service. Luxury car lines have high-end models that enhance the prestige of the entire line. However, they are priced to encourage sales of the more profitable middle and lower end.

Differential pricing. Charge each customer or each segment what each will pay. Car sellers try to get the best deal they can from everyone. Golf courses offer discounts to local citizens. Financial planning fees often relate to income level. Be careful you don't violate federal or state price discrimination laws.

Fixed, then variable pricing. Institute a just-to-get-started charge, followed by a variable charge. Taxi fares and phone service are examples. This pricing technique works well when your fixed costs are high per order or for setup.

Price point pricing. Price just below important thresholds for the buyer to give a perception of lower price. Books sold for $19.95, suits sold for $299, and houses sold for $295,000 are examples.

Odd pricing. Use pricing figures that end in 5, 7, and 9 for psychological reasons. Consumers tend to round down a price of $39.95 to $39, rather than rounding it up to $40, and they see it in the $30 price range rather than the $40 price range.

Markdown and sale pricing. Consider markdowns in price and special sales when inventory levels become too high. This could be the result of overbuying, seasonal or shopworn merchandise, or misjudged customer response. It could also be the result of poor personal selling, lack of promotion, or competition lowering the price. Avoid being left with items that will not sell. The longer they stay, the higher the storage and insurance costs, and the less room you have for current, salable merchandise.

Multiple pricing. This is the practice of promoting a number of units for a single price, such as two for five dollars. This is useful primarily in low-cost, consumable products and for sales and year-end clearances.

Special group pricing. Consider giving discount prices to members of special groups, such as credit unions, professional associations, or trade groups. Other possible discounts include military, senior citizens, previous customers, volume buyers, and other merchants in the same center. Consider using a membership plan.

Special sale pricing. Consider the wording of your special offers and discounts. For example, test whether "two for one," "50 percent off," "buy one—get the second for one penny," or "buy one—get one free" work best. They all mean the same thing, but there can be dramatic differences in results.

Free add-ons and premiums pricing. Consider all the free or nominal cost items or services you might add to your basic product to substantially increase the perceived value. Free membership, multiple payment plan options, ability to pay later, and no interest charges are examples. Trial period, gifts, accessories, supplies, installation, alterations, delivery, training, upgrades, updates, consultations, inspections, estimates, exams, and evaluations are other possibilities.

Cash discount pricing. Consider giving discounts to customers who pay with cash or check today or within a very limited time, rather than thirty, sixty, or ninety days in the future. You have the money, it saves you billing and clerical costs, and it eliminates bad debts. Also consider giving discounts for paying with cash rather than credit cards. You save the premium charged by the bank.

Trade discount pricing. Everyone in the distribution channel needs and expects to have a certain margin when they purchase and resell your product. Make sure you have a logical, fair, and consistent method for pricing to the trade. This can be particularly challenging if you are selling through several different channels.

Cumulative quantity discount pricing. Consider discounts based on the customer's accumulated purchases. This encourages loyalty and continued purchases. Airline frequent flyer programs, fast-food restaurants where your tenth purchase is free, car washes where the fifth wash is free, and barbers where the seventh haircut is free are examples. Service businesses should try to incorporate this strategy. The cost is minimal, and the continued patronage is valuable. Consider using an attractive card with your name, logo, and phone number that customers keep with them. It will constantly remind them and reinforce their commitment to your business.

Noncumulative quantity discount pricing. This discount encourages purchasing more than one item per visit. The "baker's dozen," "buy three and get the fourth free," and "two for one dinner" offers are all examples. There are tremendous opportunities for service businesses to become more creative here too. The most difficult sale is the first one. Make the customer an offer for more of the same items or compatible add-ons at a great price that is impossible to ignore.

Volume packaging pricing. Slightly lowering the price per unit of measure encourages purchasing more of the item. Buying 100 pounds of cat litter, or 48 ounces of shampoo, at one time in one container are examples. This pricing technique works when packaging costs are a high portion of total product cost.

CHAPTER 9
ACTION ITEMS

Price

1. Determine a price for your product or service and justify it using value-in-use pricing.

2. Complete a mathematical analysis of your pricing that adequately compensates all distribution channels.

3. Select and describe at least five creative pricing techniques you could use for your product or service.

CHAPTER 10

Promotion: Public Relations

Grand opening extravaganza—this might be one of your first public relations attempts. You hope many more will follow. Advertising is the *promotion* method that probably first comes to mind for most people. However, advertising is only one of four major promotion categories within the marketing mix. Public relations, sales promotion, and personal selling are the other three. Many start-up businesses should put more time and energy into these techniques, and less into advertising.

This chapter highlights some of the many opportunities for building public relations and suggests ways to get publicity from the news media. It also describes some sales promotion ideas that might stimulate business. Chapter 11 covers advertising, and chapter 12 covers personal selling.

PUBLICITY POSSIBILITIES

Public relations encompasses many things. Any activity performed by your business or the people who represent your business is an opportunity for publicity. The goal is to convey a positive image through favorable impressions that eventually increase sales and profits. Obtaining favorable publicity from the news media is one public relations tool. There are also many other public relations possibilities and opportunities.

Advertising and public relations are different. The business pays directly for advertising. The business directs advertising to a specific market through a specific media with a specific message. It sells products and services, and it can have an immediate effect. However, potential customers recognize that the business pays for advertising with its own vested interest in mind. Customers don't fully believe all advertising. Some of it is misleading or untrue. Many customers swayed by advertising are not loyal to your business.

You don't pay directly for public relations, although some of the activities that generate good public relations certainly have a cost. Public relations programs are ongoing. They may not pay immediate dividends. However, they will often be more valuable than advertising in the long run. The positive image generated by good public relations, including good publicity, is more believable than that generated by advertising. The persuaded customers are more likely to remain. Public relations sells your company and the people behind your products and services.

You need both advertising and public relations. They should work consistently and synergistically for maximum benefit to your customers. This will then benefit your business.

Here are some public relations ideas to consider using in your business:

Company Culture and Customer Contact
- Honest, reliable business practices
- Generous return policy
- Friendly, courteous employees
- Pleasant telephone demeanor
- Efficient phone system
- Professionalism and neatness
- Professional decor and attire
- Professional and informational business cards and stationery
- Smiles and greetings
- Refreshments and pleasant music
- Customer testimonials
- Flexible financing options
- Regular contact with employees and their families

Business Brochure

- Lend credibility, visibility, and status to your business.
- Precisely describe your products and services.
- Emphasize benefits and differences from competitors.
- Highlight background and experience of owners and employees.
- Use separate inserts for information that will change.
- Use logos, slogans, graphics, and testimonials.
- Make it easy for prospective customers to contact you.
- Distribute the brochure appropriately.
- Ask for and act on constructive feedback.

Company Newsletter

- Maintain customer contact.
- Build rapport with customers.
- Establish and improve image.
- Allow customers to place orders.
- Demonstrate your technical knowledge and give useful ideas.
- Utilize human interest stories about customers and employees.
- Inform customers of changes in hours, services, or policies.
- Suggest new and different ways to use your products and services.
- Profile a customer or employee.
- Print testimonial letters from customers.
- Utilize a question and answer column.
- Highlight special sales and closeouts.
- Ask for customer feedback.
- Utilize information response cards.
- Keep customers informed of new laws and regulations.

Special Events

- Grand opening
- Expansions and new locations

- New products or services
- Open houses
- Office or facility tours
- Theme celebrations
- Holiday parties
- Anniversary parties
- Charity fund-raising events
- Contests and giveaways
- Samples and demonstrations
- Fairs and trade shows
- Invitation-only events
- Seminars, lectures, and workshops

Speaking Engagements

- Television and radio news and talk shows
- Service clubs
- Civic and community organizations
- Professional and industry organizations
- Colleges and universities

Writing Engagements

- Articles
- Columns
- Computer databases
- Research reports
- Political and governmental papers

Generating Publicity

- News releases
- Public service announcements
- Letters to the editor
- Reprints of articles and publicity
- Tie-ins to a current news event
- Analyses and predictions
- Timely and newsworthy statistics
- Conducting and publicizing surveys
- Tie-ins to community projects
- Creating and presenting awards
- Localizing a national news item
- Announcing hires and promotions
- Locating and using a memorable spokesperson
- Doing something unusual or incredible

Memberships and Affiliations

- Clubs and trade associations
- Chambers of Commerce
- Professional associations
- Political offices
- Committee involvement
- Religious, athletic, and social groups

Charitable Contributions

- Employees volunteering time
- Employees contributing cash
- Company donations of money or property
- Company donations of time, space, and name
- Sponsorship and support

Participation in Community Events

- Sponsorship of company athletic teams
- Sponsorship of noncompany athletic teams
- School project or club sponsorships
- Community fund-raisers
- Community projects
- Community political involvement

NEWS RELEASES

When you or your company does anything newsworthy, send a news release to the appropriate media. Make sure it is *news* and not just an *ad*. Use your creativity to find a news angle if necessary. Neatly and accurately type it. Follow these basic rules when preparing the story:

- Type double or triple spaced, one side only, on 8 ½-by-11-inch paper. Avoid paper that smears.
- In the upper left corner, type your business name, address, and then your own name and telephone number. This will identify both the business and you as the news source. The editor will have no trouble reaching you if there are questions about the story. Put the date in the upper right corner.
- Put the release date a few spaces from the contact identification. Examples include *For Immediate Release*, *Release at Your Convenience*, and *For Release*

after April 3. Follow up with a phone call if it is time-sensitive. If you are giving an exclusive, let the recipient know by typing *Exclusive* above the release information. Don't give the story to any other news source.

- Use an interest-grabbing headline to catch the attention of the reader. Address the release to the specific department and the specific editor if possible.
- Start typing the story about one-third of the way down the page. Keep the story as brief as possible. Use short sentences. Head all following pages with the business name and the page number.
- Answer the journalistic questions raised by who, what, where, when, why, and how. If the release needs an explanation, attach a short note.
- Indicate that release continues to the next page by using "-more-" at the bottom of the page. At the top of each page, type the headline again and add the page number. Try to keep the release to no more than two pages. Indicate the end of your release by using "# # #" or "-30-."
- The telephone is a beneficial tool in news gathering. However, it's not necessary to call the newspaper to ask whether you can send in a story. Simply send it. Additionally, don't expect an editor or reporter to take your routine story over the phone.
- Give the full name of your business in the story and fully identify it. Don't assume that readers know the business.
- Consider the market served by the paper, magazine, radio station, television station, or other media. Prominently mention those aspects or angles at the beginning of the story, and highlight them throughout.
- Don't begin a story with a time, day, date, or name.
- Don't submit carbon copies or duplicated copies that are impossible to decipher.
- Don't submit copy typed in all capital letters. If you're unsure about capitalization, the journalist will correct any errors.

- Use a person's full name the first time you mention it in a story. After that first mention, use the person's last name alone. Rarely use nicknames or the terms "Mr., Mrs., and Ms."
- Use *women* instead of *ladies*, and use *men* instead of *gentlemen*.
- Don't use glowing tributes, flowery descriptives, or similar adjectives that constitute opinion. News stories are objective and do not contain editorials.
- Remember that names make news. Don't leave out the names of anyone pertinent to the story. At the same time, avoid long lists of names when possible.
- Make sure the release is *news* and is relevant to the subject and geographic coverage of the media selected. Keep the *plugs* for products and services to a minimum.
- Remember the theory that a picture is worth a thousand words. Consider furnishing a picture or requesting a media photographer for your event. If you take your own photograph, make sure it is sharp, black and white, and preferably at least five by seven inches.
- Take interesting photographs instead of the run-of-the-mill poses people see and use every day. Try to have no more than three people in a photo. Try to have them doing something. Describe the photograph, and identify the people from left to right by typing or clearly printing a cutline for the photograph. Paste it onto the photograph and fold it back. Never write or type on the back of a photograph.
- Cultivate good long-term relationships with members of the media. Be honest and fair. Don't play one department, one newspaper, or one reporter against another.
- Don't go over someone's head except in the most extreme case. Don't exaggerate the importance of a news release. Don't throw your weight around. Don't leave information holes in your news release.

- Don't complain if they rewrite your release. Don't complain if they cut it or leave it out completely. Don't get angry and don't demand a retraction for unimportant details. Don't send lavish gifts, don't lean on newspaper friends, and don't threaten anyone.
- Be as helpful as possible and do as much work as possible to make the reporter's job easier. Trust reporters to honor your off-the-record comments.
- Honor exclusive stories and give credit where and when due. Thank people who have been helpful. Politely tell a reporter if something is incorrect.
- Take an interest in the media. Subscribe to and read all publications where you send releases.

Sales Promotion

Sales promotion activities are the items, other than advertising, public relations, and personal selling, that stimulate interest, trial, or purchase by final customers or others in the distribution channel. You can direct your sales promotion activities to consumers, distributors, or your own salespeople.

These activities are rarely the main promotion activity of a business, but they are often an effective and fun supplement to the regular promotion schedule. Here are some examples:

Sales Promotion Activities Aimed at Final Consumers

- Banners and streamers
- Samples
- Calendars
- Point-of-purchase materials
- Aisle displays and signs
- Contests and games
- Sweepstakes and lotteries
- Demonstrations
- Coupons and rebates
- Trade shows and fairs
- Trading stamps
- Low-interest financing
- Entertainment

- Trade-in allowances
- Tie-ins
- Sports sponsorship

Sales Promotion Activities Aimed at Middlemen

- Price deals and rebates
- Promotion allowances
- Sales contests
- Calendars
- Gifts and premiums
- Trade shows and fairs
- Exhibits
- Demonstrations
- Meetings
- Catalogs
- Merchandising aids
- Signs and displays

Sales Promotion Activities Aimed at Your Own Sales Force

- Contests and games
- Bonuses
- Meetings
- Portfolios
- Displays
- Sales aids
- Training materials
- Travel incentives

CHAPTER 10
ACTION ITEMS

Promotion: Public Relations

1. Select at least five public relations ideas to implement in your business.

2. Write a press release for your grand opening, emphasizing the news angle.

3. Select at least five sales promotion activities to implement in your business.

CHAPTER 11

Promotion: Advertising

Free Mercedes Benz! Yes, with the right headline and the right offer you can dramatically increase customers and sales through advertising. Done right, it can be your most effective and immediate promotion technique. However, it can be a great waste of time and money if not done right.

For many, advertising is synonymous with marketing. It is not. Remember that marketing is the complete process of segmenting the market, targeting your ideal customer, and implementing the full marketing mix to satisfy that customer. Advertising is only one of four promotion types. Promotion is only one of the 4 Ps of the marketing mix. Advertising is important, but keep it in perspective. For many small and start-up businesses, other promotion methods may be more effective in the long term. They almost certainly will be more economical.

This chapter describes the main reasons to advertise and discusses the characteristics of effective advertising. It also illustrates the main elements of a great ad and highlights your main media choices.

FEATURES AND BENEFITS

There are many specific reasons to advertise, but all fall within the three major categories of informing, persuading, and reminding.

For most small and start-up businesses, the main reason to advertise is to persuade the customer to buy their products or services or to buy more of them. You may need to inform the customer of all the benefits to persuade them. However, informing or reminding by themselves are not the best use of your advertising dollar. Large companies with unlimited budgets may be able to do this, but you need to show a specific and verifiable rate of return on your advertising investment.

Here are some characteristics of effective ads and some suggestions for you to consider:

- Know the main objective of the ad and stick with it.
- Direct the ad at your target market.
- Choose the right medium for the ad.
- Be informative, truthful, credible, and convincing.
- Arouse emotions such as hope, admiration, or fear.
- Catch the prospect's attention with a powerful headline and a good lead sentence.
- Stress the benefits over the features.
- Use an appropriate tone and powerful words such as *free, save, new, easy, you,* and *guarantee.*
- Remember that advertising is "salesmanship multiplied." Even though many people may see or hear your ad, each one is seeing or hearing it individually.
- Always test elements of the ad. Try to find a better way. Test headline, offer, placement, price, media, and so forth.
- Make sure you can track and measure the results of your ads.
- Make the ad easy, simple, and attractive with photos, illustrations, and enough "white space."
- Make the ad large enough to see or long enough to hear.
- Repeat the ad, repeat the benefits, and repeat the phone number.
- Use a logo or a theme for quick recognition.
- Use third-party endorsements of your product or service.

- Use guarantees and risk-free offers.
- Use time limits and bonuses for quick action.
- Ask for a specific response and action.
- Stay with ads that are working and change those that aren't.
- Negotiate the best deals with the media. Consider forming your own advertising agency to receive 15 percent agency discounts. Ask for remnant rates, discounts, vacant time, and space.
- Consider cooperative advertising, where others who benefit share the cost of the ad.

CREATING A GREAT AD

A great advertisement has a powerful headline to grab the potential customer's attention. It has an offer the customer can't refuse. It backs up and fortifies the offer with many benefits. It has a final clear call to action.

The headline is the most important part of the ad. It is the ad for the ad. If it doesn't grab the prospect's attention, the rest of the ad is immaterial.

The sole purpose of a headline is to persuade prospects to continue reading the ad or sales letter. The headline must grab their attention and pull them into your ad. Your headline should be so irresistible that it compels your reader to find out more.

All ads should have a headline. Here are some rules to follow when writing headlines:

- Appeal to the reader's self-interest. Communicate the strongest benefit and answer the question, What's in it for the reader? Get to your point fast.
- Concentrate on attracting the attention of your target prospect. Forget everyone else. You don't need to appeal to everyone.
- Deliver a clear and understandable message. Many people read only the headline. Ensure that you have a complete statement that compels them to continue reading.
- Make it simple, newsworthy, and believable.
- Don't try to be too clever or too humorous. Stress benefits.

- Include powerful words such as *free, easy, save, how to, announcing, you, new,* and *discover* if they fit what you are communicating.
- Use specifics rather than generalities. Specifics are more believable.
- Arouse curiosity and promise benefits.
- Speak directly to the reader, one reader at a time.
- Test two headlines against each other to determine which pulls the best response.
- Use uppercase and lowercase letters for your headlines. Consider using quotation marks. These techniques make reading easier.
- Write many possible headlines before settling on one.

There are several headline types you can use. Here are some ideas and examples of each:

News headline. If your product or service offers something newsworthy, announce it in your headline. Use words such as *new, announcing, introducing, now, at last.* Example: New Diet Burns Fat While You Sleep.

Guarantee headline. State a desirable benefit and guarantee results or other benefits. Example: Stop Smoking in Two Weeks or Your Money Back.

How-to headline. Promise your prospects a source for information, advice, and solutions to their problems. Example: How to Buy Real Estate with No Money Down.

Benefit headline. Offer a powerful, compelling benefit that people can't easily obtain elsewhere. Example: Even If You've Had Credit Problems in the Past, You Can Qualify for Our Loans.

Question headline. Know your target audience well, and focus on your prospect's self-interest by asking a question they want answered. Example: Can You Pass the Entrepreneur Success Test?

Reason why headline. Give your prospects specific reasons why they should read your ad. Use specific facts and numbers. Example: 99 Ways to Improve Your Offer.

Testimonial headline. Use a customer testimonial to sell your product or service by letting a satisfied third party talk about the benefits. Example: I Lost 35 Pounds on the Weight Watchers Diet.

Command headline. Encourage action by offering your prospect a benefit that will help them. Start with an action verb. Example: Stop Worrying and Start Living.

Here are some of the most powerful and persuasive words to use in your headlines and offers:

Save	Health	Love	Proven
Discover	You	Easy	Results
Safety	Guarantee	Money	New
Free	Sale	Introducing	Benefits
Alternative	Now	Win	Gain
Happy	Trustworthy	Good-looking	Proud
Comfortable	Announcing	Right	Security
Fun	Value	Advice	Wanted
Bargain	How To	Life	Success
Amazing	At Last	Breakthrough	Do You
Facts	Here	Immediate	Magic
Powerful	Quick	Secrets of	Surprising
Suddenly	Sensational	Remarkable	Startling
Revolutionary	Miracle	Offer	Challenge

Once you've caught prospects' attention with a powerful headline, encourage them to continue reading by creating an irresistible offer. Each sentence and each paragraph should build on the preceding one, pulling the reader through the whole ad. Build on the interest and excitement created by the headline.

Here are some ideas for more powerful offers:

- Emphasize the word *free* and repeat it when possible.
- Clearly state your offer in the headline or a subhead.
- Use subheads, paragraphs, and white space.
- Start the body copy with a large initial letter.
- Use a short first paragraph to pull in the reader.
- Write in the active voice and use active verbs.
- Make every sentence lead to the next sentence.
- Write concisely to one person.
- Avoid jargon.
- Use sufficient-size type, generally at least 9-point.
- Use serif type to make reading easier.

- Use uppercase and lowercase. All caps are difficult to read.
- Use arrowheads, bullets, and asterisks.
- Don't use white-on-black reverse type.
- Show pictures of your product or service in action.
- Include third-party testimonials.
- Differentiate your ad from others in the same media.
- Add urgency to your offer.
- Experiment with borders, colors, sizes, and placement.
- Tell your full story, even if it is lengthy.
- Use short words, short sentences, and short paragraphs.

Consider these incentives to spice up your offers:

- Bonuses
- Guarantees
- Free samples
- Contests
- Gifts
- Free reports
- Free shipping
- Trade-ins
- Memberships
- Risk-free trials

Emphasize the benefits to the prospect of using your product or service to persuade them to take advantage of the offer. Put yourself in the customer's shoes. They want, need, and buy *benefits*, not features. Make sure your ad speaks to the customers and addresses their wants.

Review the major needs and wants your product or service is trying to satisfy. Pound them home through the headline, offer, and benefits. Be consistent. Don't be afraid to repeat powerful points.

The last element of a great ad is a clear and powerful call for action. Now that you have the prospects' attention, and the offer and benefits interest and excite them, call them to action. Persuade them to act now before they change their mind, forget, or go on to something else.

Here are a few ways to encourage immediate action:

- Use a "hook" such as
  - Special report
  - Sample

- Free trial
- Premium
- Introductory price
- Time payments
- Put a time limit on your offer.
- Stress the fact that you have a limited supply.
- Feature complete satisfaction or a complete refund with no questions asked.
- If you are going to raise the price, emphasize that point and specify a date.
- If you are going to reduce the price, emphasize that point and stress the desirability of taking advantage of the offer.
- Stress what your prospects gain by acting immediately.
- Stress what they lose by not owning your product.
- Use a twenty-four-hour, toll-free number and accept credit cards.

Close your ad by telling your readers or listeners what to do. Give them something to call for, write for, stop by for, or do. Here are some possible closings to consider:

Act now! Send for details	Ask for free report
Be first to qualify	Get started today
It's free! Act now!	No obligation! Call now!
Offer limited! Call today	Order now! Don't delay!
Rush name for details	See before you buy
Send for free report	Send no money

MEDIA CHOICES

Choose the best media to get your message to your target market. Knowing the demographics of your customers and their reading, listening, and viewing habits is essential.

Media choices vary with location and with changes in technology. Continue to test and compare to see if better choices become available. Measure the results of all advertising campaigns. Break them down to a return on investment that you can use to compare campaigns and strategies.

Here are some of the traditional media choices with comments on the suitability and advantages and disadvantages of each:

Newspaper

Suitability: Useful for all general retailers; covers single community or metropolitan area; zoned editions sometimes available; audience is generally male, older, with higher income and education.

Advantages: Wide circulation, location segmentation, frequent publication, short lead time, and credibility. Favorable for cooperative advertising, volume and frequency discounts, and assistance for copy and layout.

Disadvantages: Nonselective audience, limited exposure, expensive, short life, limited reproduction quality.

Shopper

Suitability: Useful for neighborhood retailers and service businesses; covers most local consumer households.

Advantages: Consumer orientation.

Disadvantages: Consumers don't always read giveaways or take them seriously.

Yellow Pages

Suitability: Useful for service providers, retailers of brand-name items, and highly specialized retailers. It covers the geographic area serving active shoppers.

Advantages: Users are in the market and ready to buy. This is often the first and only place a prospect may look.

Disadvantages: Limited to active shoppers; expensive.

Magazine

Suitability: Local magazines useful for restaurants, entertainment businesses, specialty shops, and mail-order businesses. Trade and national magazines available; zoned editions sometimes available; appeals to better-educated and more affluent.

Advantages: Delivery of a loyal, special-interest audience; high-quality production; volume and frequency discounts; credibility; reprint value. Several people often read the same issue.

Disadvantages: Limited audience, long lead time, limited control over placement, expensive.

Radio

Suitability: Useful for businesses catering to identifiable listening groups such as teens, homemakers, and commuters; definable market area and demographics; works well in combination with other media.

Advantages: Target demographic and geographic segments; audio capability; relatively low cost; short lead time; reaches large audience; reaches audience in cars; remnant (unsold) space rates, discounts, and bartering are all possible.

Disadvantages: Limited to audio; short life of message; subject to distractions while listening. Business must buy time consistently to be of value.

Television

Suitability: Useful for sellers of products or services with wide appeal. Specialized cable channels can target a more specialized audience. It appeals to younger age group that is less oriented to print. It covers a definable market geographic area. Television is authoritative and influential.

Advantages: Dramatic impact, wide market coverage, visual and audio capabilities, short lead time, low cost per exposure, high prestige.

Disadvantages: High cost of time and production, requires production specialists, short exposure time.

Direct Mail

Suitability: Useful for new and expanding businesses and for businesses that use coupons and catalogs. Demographic lists control audience and coverage.

Advantages: Personalized approach to an audience of good prospects; flexibility and control in reaching target market; no clutter from competing ads; stimulate action; easy to test and measure; useful for building a database; equalizer for small business.

Disadvantages: Easily thrown away as "junk mail"; high cost of lists and mailings.

Outdoor

Suitability: Useful for amusement and tourist businesses and for brand-name retailers. It covers auto drivers in neighborhood or metropolitan area.

Advantages: Dominant size, frequency of exposure, relatively inexpensive, message works twenty-four hours per day.

Disadvantages: Limited message possible; cannot reach well-defined target markets; clutter of many signs; short exposure time.

Transit

Suitability: Useful for businesses along transit routes, especially those appealing to wage earners. It covers area served by transit system and appeals to employees, shoppers, and pedestrians using or viewing the system.

Advantages: Repetition and length of exposure.

Disadvantages: Limited audience.

Consider forming your own in-house advertising agency. Media outlets traditionally pay agencies a 15 percent commission for placing ads with them. They figure the 15 percent in the price of the advertising, so it's irrelevant whether they pay it to you or to an agency. You can save 15 percent on all advertising you place in traditional media. Simply print some letterhead and insertion orders for your new agency. When placing an ad, request the standard 15 percent agency commission.

If you're a retailer or manufacturer, always consider cooperative advertising. Cooperative, or co-op, advertising is a way to allow others who are benefiting from your advertising to share in the cost. Retailers who are advertising specific brands of merchandise should ask the manufacturer to pay for some of the advertising. Manufacturers who are advertising their own products should consider mentioning local retailers who sell or service their product. Persuade the retailers to contribute to the advertising cost. Be clear, fair, and legal with any co-op advertising program.

Consider bartering for ad space as well as for other products and services your business needs. The advertising industry uses bartering extensively. Because unused air time or newspaper space is worthless, media are often willing to trade time or space for your products or services. It won't happen unless you ask.

CHAPTER 11
ACTION ITEMS

Promotion: Advertising

1. Design a complete Yellow Pages display listing or a newspaper ad that emphasizes the listed characteristics of effective ads.

2. Write three possible headlines for the ad you developed.

3. Select and explain the three most appropriate media for you to concentrate your advertising.

CHAPTER 12

Promotion: Personal Selling

Selling skills will be one of the most lucrative and beneficial long-term abilities you can develop. Personal selling skills are important in every business. Their proper use in combination with other promotion methods can dramatically increase your business success.

As owner of the business, you will continually need to sell your business, yourself, and your product or service. Bankers, investors, suppliers, customers, and others are all recipients of your selling skills. As the business grows, you will likely use employees or independent contractors to sell for you. It is crucial to hire and train the best candidates.

The need and importance of personal selling for specific products or services varies with the type of business. Some businesses, like real estate and automobile sales, use advertising to *inform* and *interest* the customer. They then use personal selling skills to add details, answer questions, and consummate the purchase. Sales of low-cost consumer products may rely almost completely on advertising with little or no personal selling needed. Many small retail and service businesses do little advertising. They rely predominantly on personal selling and public relations.

If you plan to use independent sales representatives, contact the Manufacturers' Agents National Association at (714) 859-4040. Request a listing of their publications and a membership packet.

In its most basic form, personal selling consists of the **AIDA** formula: Get the prospect's **Attention**. Create **Interest** in the product. Build the prospect's **Desire** to own the product. Finally, persuade the prospect to take **Action**.

Good salespeople need to be skilled in three distinct areas: product and customer knowledge, personal skills, and specific selling strategies and tactics. This chapter highlights those three areas.

COMPANY, PRODUCT, AND CUSTOMER KNOWLEDGE

Successful selling requires extensive company, product, and customer knowledge. After asking questions to assess the customer's needs, a substantial part of the sales presentation involves giving information about your product or service that relates to those needs. You may have aroused the prospect's interest with your advertising, a customer's referral, or your initial contact. The prospect's first motivation, at this point, is the need for more information. You should provide it. In many cases, especially when selling services, information about your company may be even more important than information about your service.

Be prepared to answer all questions with accuracy and confidence. When you show confidence in your company and product, your prospect is also more likely to show confidence. Company and product knowledge build respect. Respect leads to repeat sales and referrals.

Know your product and fully understand what it can do for your prospective buyer. This knowledge positions you to overcome any reasons for not buying. Be able to clearly explain the product features and, more important, the product benefits to the customer. Practice translating the features into customer benefits.

How do you and those who sell for you acquire the essential product knowledge? Here are some ideas:

- Become directly involved in researching and developing new products and services.
- Attend and participate in formal training and sales meetings.

- Fully examine and understand your product, and be able to properly demonstrate it.
- Read all of the manufacturing and sales literature related to your product.
- Read and understand all contracts and any other documents that the customer might question.
- Visit the manufacturer or distributor, and understand the manufacturing and distribution process.
- Talk to other people, including cooperative competitors, who sell the same product or service.
- Subscribe to professional and trade journals. Read relevant articles in magazines, journals, and newspapers.
- Talk to the service and repair people.
- Use the product yourself.
- Follow up, survey customers, and listen to what they have to say.
- Read about and study competing products and services.

PERSONAL SALES SKILLS

Besides superior company, product, and customer knowledge, the best salespeople possess the following personal skills and qualities:

- They are team players and are coachable.
- They are always prompt and well prepared.
- They are constantly learning and looking for better ways to sell.
- They write down and achieve worthwhile goals.
- They pay attention to details.
- They have good work and time-management habits.
- They are self-confident and have a positive attitude.
- They are creative and have a good sense of humor.
- They are reliable and keep their commitments.
- They display conviction and enthusiasm.
- They are sincere and honest.
- They believe in their company and product.

- They play the role of expert advisor rather than salesperson.
- They are excellent listeners.
- They never argue with a customer.
- They are empathetic and courteous.
- They focus on the customer's needs, place themselves in the customer's shoes, and see things from the customer's point of view.
- They are knowledgeable about the competition, but they never put down the competition.
- They know the strengths and weaknesses of the competition.
- They are physically fit and emotionally stable.
- They take pride in their appearance and dress appropriately for their market.
- They shake hands firmly and practice good eye contact.
- They speak clearly, and they are aware of vocal quality and change.
- They see failure and rejection as learning experiences and useful feedback.
- They don't take rejection personally.
- They desire long-term relationships with customers.
- They follow up with the customer, and they act as a valuable resource for the customer.
- They return for repeat orders.
- They deliver more value than the customer expects.

How many of these statements describe you? How can you find people to work and sell for you that reflect these traits?

SELLING STRATEGIES AND TACTICS

Knowledge and personal skills make up two of the three legs on the personal selling needs list. Good training, along with proper utilization of proven selling strategies and tactics, is the third leg. Practice is imperative.

The personal selling skills you need to learn and master are

1. Prospecting for future customers
2. Making original contact with the prospect
3. Qualifying the prospect

4. Making the presentation
5. Handling concerns and objections
6. Closing the sale
7. Obtaining referrals and additional sales

Prospecting

Before you can make a sale, you need to find potential customers. This requires prospecting. Many entrepreneurs dread prospecting. Many don't do it at all. Others don't do it well and consistently. Down the road, if all works well, your business should survive and prosper on repeat business and referrals. However, start-ups probably need some aggressive prospecting to develop business.

Here are some methods to find prospects:

Prior and current satisfied customers. Your easiest sale could be prior and current customers who may need more or additional products and services. You need to ask and suggest, and you need to keep in contact with all of them.

Cold calls. Knock on doors and call on the telephone. It's a numbers game and the rejection rate is high. Learn to deal with rejection. Don't take it personally.

Public speaking and seminars. Get in front of people. Entertain and educate them. This is a great way for service professionals to develop business.

Recommendations. Ask family, friends, social contacts, and business contacts for the names of likely prospects.

Referred leads. Ask satisfied customers to provide names of interested parties. This is probably the best source of leads. Consider offering incentives. Develop the mind-set that each customer represents one hundred qualified referrals. You'll be sure to treat every customer well.

Ads or direct mail leads. Use direct mail or other media advertising to obtain inquiries about your products and services.

Newspaper and trade magazine articles. Keep your eyes open for events and items of interest to your business. This could include birth announcements, engagements, social events, new jobs, new businesses, promotions, and feature stories on businesses and people.

Telephone and city directories and indexes. If your target market is a defined group, locate your prospects in the Yellow Pages or other compiled listings.

Civic, trade, and professional associations. Obtain membership rosters by joining, working through an acquaintance who is a member, or purchasing the list.

Support groups. Business resource and networking groups can be good sources for potential business.

Centers of influence. Prominent people in your community, such as politicians, bankers, lawyers, ministers, and executives may be excellent sources of qualified referrals. Make sure they know about or use your products and services and are confident in your abilities.

Purchased prospect lists. You can buy or rent mailing and telephone lists of almost every imaginable group of prospects with certain characteristics. Contact a list broker under "Mailing Lists" in the Yellow Pages, or review *Standard Rate and Data Service* (SRDS) at your library.

Fairs, trade shows, and conventions. Arrange for a booth or table at appropriate events. Have all visitors register for a prize drawing. When the event is over, follow up on your prospect leads.

Original Contact

The original contact with a prospect can be by telephone, mail, or in person. Each makes a different impression, and each has its advantages and disadvantages. Consider your ability to receive feedback from the prospect and your ability to reach some degree of resolution when choosing the most appropriate method. Often you may decide to use some combination of all three contact methods.

Letters serve well as introductions, especially if they include a third-party endorsement. Letters can secure appointments, answer questions, reach busy people, and follow up on a sales call. They can provide updates and stimulate business. They can strengthen trust, maintain interest, and keep the lines of communication open.

Don't use form letters. Type or word-process a personalized letter on quality stationery. Use a strong introductory sentence. Break up the text in short, well-focused paragraphs with short sentences. Clarify the benefits to the customer of meeting and speaking with you. Make sure there are no typos or spelling errors. Include supplemental information such as a brochure. Indicate when you will follow up with a call.

Phone calls can be the most cost-effective way to make initial contact with a prospect. Use the telephone to reach customers and prospects to schedule appointments. You can also answer and ask questions. The primary disadvantage is your sole reliance on the verbal and vocal aspects of communication.

Effective phone calling requires that you test your vocal quality. Eliminate background noise. Be very organized and prepared. Call at the most appropriate time. Learn to work well with secretaries and other screeners. Observe telephone etiquette. Listen effectively.

At times, use an in-person meeting as an introductory call. Use it to gather information on your prospect. You must know and trust each other before you can transact business. Be sure to clearly introduce yourself and your business. Establish the purpose for the call. Start to uncover needs by asking appropriate questions. Eventually, propose a solution. Make sure you smile, maintain good eye contact, and shake hands firmly. Remain calm.

Qualifying

Make sure to qualify your prospect before starting your presentation or demonstration. Time is a salesperson's most valuable commodity. You want to spend that time presenting and demonstrating to people who will and can buy your product or service. Don't waste your time with those who won't or can't buy.

Here are the basic steps to qualify prospects before starting your presentation or demonstration:

1. Tactfully determine who will make the final buying decision.
2. Find out what products or services they are currently using that relate to the needs you are trying to solve.
3. Find out what they like most about the current products or services they are using.
4. Find out what they would like to see changed or improved in the current products or services.
5. If you can meet all their needs, will they proceed?
6. Probe gently for product, service, and budget concerns, giving them choices and ranges.

Making the Presentation

Your presentation or demonstration technique depends on your product or service and your prospect. Regardless, be well prepared in all cases. Make sure you develop an opening statement with a benefit that fits the prospects' needs. Rehearse the flow of your presentation, making sure it is well-paced and brief. Use an introduction, presentation, and summary.

Prepare any brochures, catalogs, or personalized information that you plan to leave with the prospect. Prepare a list of questions you intend to ask. Prepare answers to possible objections. Have examples available of how your product or service assisted in similar situations. Provide relevant third-party testimonials.

Tailor your presentation technique to the personality of the prospect. Your prospecting, initial contact, and qualifying steps should give you some insight into the person. By looking at only two dimensions of behavior you can determine a person's dominant behavioral style. Use the two dimensions of openness and directness to classify people as *relaters, socializers, thinkers*, or *directors*. Graphically, the four styles look as follows:

The Four Styles of Behavior

OPEN
(Relationship oriented)

The Relater — We're all in this together, so let's work as a team

The Socializer — Let me tell you what happened to me.

INDIRECT (Slow pace) ——————————— (Fast pace) DIRECT

The Thinker — Can you provide documentation for your claims?

The Director — I want it done right, and I want it done now!

SELF-CONTAINED
(Task oriented)

Classifying someone in a behavioral style requires you to make two important decisions:

➠ Are they open or self-contained?
➠ Are they direct or indirect?

Openness is the ease with which a person shows emotions and responds to other people. A very open person is willing to share thoughts and feelings and jump into new relationships. A self-contained person would remain aloof. Self-contained people do not mind being alone and frequently prefer it. Open people are more people-oriented. Self-contained people are more task-oriented.

Directness refers to the amount of control a person attempts to exert over people and situations. It often reflects their need for power. The amount of effort a person uses to gain control also reflects attitudes toward risk taking and change.

Maintain flexibility in your own style so that you can tailor your presentation or demonstration to meet the needs and personality of the prospect. Each of the four basic behavioral styles, and all the substyles and combinations that occur in the world, require a different approach. The good salesperson understands this and adjusts accordingly.

During your presentation, make sure you keep the prospect mentally and physically involved. Ask involvement questions and give them simple things to do. Maintain control and handle any concerns or interruptions appropriately. Emphasize benefits. Use effective visual aids, testimonial letters, printed materials, and models whenever possible. Listen to the prospect. Let the prospect physically handle the product.

Recognize the power and effect of words and language. Create positive buying emotions by substituting the words on the right for those on the left:

Price	=	Total investment
Down payment	=	Initial investment
Monthly payment	=	Monthly investment
Contract	=	Agreement, paperwork
Buy	=	Own
Sign	=	Okay, authorize, approve
Deal	=	Opportunity

Appointment	=	Visit
Objections	=	Areas of concern
Sell or sold	=	Get involved
Prospects	=	Future customers
Looker	=	Researcher
Back order	=	Fortunate oversell situation
Customers	=	People we serve

Use powerful and persuasive words in your presentation, such as those listed in chapter 11, to build desire in the prospect.

Handling Objections

Properly handling objections, or areas of concern, can make the sale. Never argue with prospects, and never attack them personally when overcoming the objection. Try to maneuver them into answering their own objections. It will be more believable to them, and it will become a reason to own.

The six steps to properly handle objections are

1. Listen carefully. Do not interrupt.
2. Feed the objection back to ensure that you understand it and hopefully to get them to answer it.
3. Ask them to elaborate on the objection and give more specifics. Make sure the stated objection is the real objection. If not, probe to find the real objection.
4. Answer the objection sincerely and honestly. Anticipate all possible objections. Have prepared responses to common objections.
5. Confirm the answer. Confirm that you satisfied their objection.
6. Move on to the next step of your presentation.

Closing

If everything has gone well until now, but you don't close the sale, it is all for naught. *Closing* is the culmination of the selling process. Everything has led up to this. Don't stop now. Closing is the traditional word used in selling. However, avoid it in your discussions with the prospect. It sounds harsh and one-sided. *Confirming the sale* is a better term to use.

Specific closing techniques are the subject of entire books. Read and study some of the techniques, and tailor the most appropriate ones to your situation. Books and tapes by Brian Tracy, Zig Ziglar, and Tom Hopkins provide some great suggestions on specific language and techniques. Taking classes on selling and closing, and joining speaking groups like Toastmasters, give you opportunities to practice and perfect your skills.

This section does not discuss specific closing techniques. However, some closing basics to keep in mind include

- Become aware of buying signals. Don't ignore them and merely continue on with your presentation. It's time to close.
- Periodically test the prospect's interest by using trial closes to determine if the prospect is ready to buy.
- Use an appropriate closing technique for the situation. Have several possible closes practiced and perfected.
- Don't talk past the close. Once you've made an attempt to close, don't say anything until the prospect responds.
- Don't give up if you receive a no. It may mean you have an objection you still need to address. Address it and try again.
- Support the customer's buying decision. Give more than expected and reassure the customer regularly to reduce buyer remorse.
- Work toward win-win situations.
- Learn from the experience. Keep in contact.

Post Closing

After you confirm the sale, consider these additional ideas before terminating the meeting. There may be additional products or services that go well with the product or service just sold. Discuss this with the customer. Provide an incentive to purchase them now. Ask the customer for names of friends, relatives, or business acquaintances who might benefit from your product or service. Don't be pushy, but remember that such qualified leads are your best future prospects.

Remember that the lifetime value of a customer greatly exceeds any one sale. Make sure your first priority is to satisfy the customer's needs, not to make a sale. Give customers more than they ask for and more than they expect. Follow up regularly and keep in contact with them. Educate them about the benefits of your products and services. Let them know you appreciate their patronage and their referrals.

CHAPTER 12
ACTION ITEMS

Promotion: Personal Selling

1. Determine your most appropriate prospects and explain how to best approach them.

2. Determine and explain the steps to properly qualify your prospects.

3. Determine and explain how you would handle two of the most probable objections.

CHAPTER 13

Determining Financial Needs and Resources

Money problems are not the most common cause of business failure. Nonetheless, starting a business undercapitalized is a recipe for disaster. You may have a great idea, a ready market, and great people, but if you run out of funds before the firm turns profitable, you will be out of business.

Remember that marketing is still the most important key to your business success. You must have a good product or service and an identifiable target market. Use the 4 Ps of the marketing mix (product, place, price, promotion) to reach and convince your prospective customers. Marketing is the foundation of your business, but marketing alone is not enough. Properly determining and covering your financial needs is necessary for long-term survival.

Estimating total capital needs is a two-step process. Calculate the amount needed to open the doors and be ready for business. Calculate the amount needed to cover cash operating expenses in excess of cash revenues until the business reaches the break-even point (sales equal expenses). Add these two estimated amounts together to obtain the total amount you need.

Once you determine the amount of capital you need, analyze possible sources of equity and debt capital. Utilize various cash management techniques to meet such needs more efficiently.

This chapter discusses the steps in determining total capital needs and suggests some possible sources for meeting them. If you can't meet your business financial needs, reassess your decision to go into business. You may need to delay, change, rearrange, or even cancel your decision. Act wisely, not emotionally.

START-UP COSTS

Start-up costs consist of every item you must obtain, and every expense you must incur and pay for, before your business is ready to open its doors. It includes the capital needed to acquire plant and equipment such as furniture, fixtures, leasehold improvements, computers, vehicles, and signs. It also includes capital needed for deposits, advertising, supplies, inventory, and training.

Make a complete list of all items you need to acquire and pay for before the business opens. Next, think of creative ways to keep the actual cash paid out for these items to a minimum. Leasing, purchasing on an installment basis, and bartering are a few techniques. Cash is king in small business. Take all possible steps to minimize cash disbursements.

Every business is different. You need to carefully analyze your specific start-up cost needs. Small personal service businesses may have minimal requirements. Retail businesses and manufacturing businesses are likely to have substantial financial needs.

Make a list of items needed, date when needed, estimated total cost, and estimated up-front cash outlay. Here are some items to consider in your analysis:

- Inventory
- Real estate
- Office equipment
- Signs
- Automobiles and trucks
- Furniture and fixtures
- Leasehold improvements and repairs
- Advertising, publicity, and promotion
- Deposits for lease, utilities, and taxes
- Legal and accounting services

- Government licenses, fees, and taxes
- Wages and payroll taxes for training
- Outside consultants and professionals
- Architect and space planner fees
- Office supplies and software
- Prepaid rent, interest, and taxes
- Telephone system
- Yellow Pages directory advertising
- Property and liability insurance
- Fees and costs to obtain capital
- Travel and investigation expenses

Regard your start-up capital, especially amounts needed for plant and equipment, as *cautious capital*. You want to minimize the actual cash outlay for these items by using some of the funding sources and techniques discussed later. Retain most of your cash for working capital needs.

Operating Costs

Create and work with your statement of cash receipts and disbursements to best analyze your working capital needs. From the planned date of opening your doors for business, project the cash coming in to the business from collection of revenue and other sources. Project the cash going out of the business through expenses, loan repayment, and any other cash disbursements. Ignore any start-up cash balance. Don't plan to withdraw any funds for personal salary or draw for now. That will occur only when the business is self-sustaining and generating a positive cash flow.

Start the analysis with a zero balance in the first month. Next, estimate and list your projected cash in and cash out amounts for each month. Carry any negative cash balance to the starting balance of the next month so that the bottom line of each month shows the cumulative positive or negative cash flow. Carry out the analysis as long as the negative cumulative cash flow balance increases. When it starts to reverse itself, and you are confident this is a permanent trend, you can end the analysis. The largest negative cumulative cash balance indicates the amount of cash you need to cover your working capital needs. This amount will allow you to survive long enough to break even and start generating positive cash flow.

Cash in consists of cash sales, collections from credit sales, and debt or equity cash contributions. Projecting sales is the most difficult part of your business and financial plan. It is guesswork, but make it educated guesswork based on your market analysis, competitive analysis, and your primary and secondary market research. Spend the necessary time on this portion, especially if you hope to convince outside parties such as bankers and investors.

Cash out consists of normal operating expenses and any continuing payments related to financed or leased start-up costs. Don't omit anything. Create a cushion for the always unexpected costs that appear.

Here are typical expense categories to consider:

- Ongoing purchases of inventory
- Salaries, wages, and payroll taxes
- Workers' compensation
- Fringe benefits
- Outside services
- Office supplies
- Repairs and maintenance
- Advertising and promotion
- Automobile and travel
- Legal and accounting
- Rent and pass-through charges
- Telephone and answering service
- Utilities
- Insurance
- Interest and principal
- Equipment lease payments
- Capital purchases
- Taxes
- Bank charges
- Commissions
- Delivery and freight
- Janitorial and cleaning
- Postage and printing
- Meals and entertainment
- Tools and uniforms
- Security
- Licenses and permits
- Education and training
- Dues and subscriptions

Chapter 18 describes and illustrates the cash flow statement. Prepare your own analysis for the expenses just as you did for sales. There are some good guidelines for estimating expenses that can assist you. Dun & Bradstreet annually publishes *Key Business Ratios*. Robert Morris Associates publishes *RMA Annual Statement Studies*. Both are excellent sources for determining average expense ratios and other financial analysis ratios classified by SIC code. Chapter 18 contains a more thorough discussion.

FINANCIAL RESOURCES

This section highlights the alternative types of financing available to businesses. Not all will apply to you, but several are certain to provide some great new ideas. There are many variations of each idea. Perhaps the specific idea mentioned may not apply, but a related approach might work perfectly. Keep your mind and your options open.

Some of the alternatives deal with equity (ownership) investments. Other alternatives deal with debt (loan) investments. Still others deal with mere deferral of payment of expenses or acceleration of receipt of income. Some use combinations of these different financing methods. This list is merely a starting point for the creative entrepreneur.

New businesses are inherently risky. Think about how you will explain and justify the risk and reward ratio to prospective investors, lenders, suppliers, and customers. Emphasize a good business idea backed up by experienced management and a well-written, thorough business plan.

Determine how much money you need, and what it's needed for, before you search for financing. Your answers must be clear, confident, and backed up by good information to increase your chances for success. Don't underestimate the amount of money and financing needed to start a business.

Additionally, calculate the amount of your projected living expenses during the start-up period. You may not be able to take money out of the business, but you must clarify how you plan to pay for personal living expenses during this time.

Here are twenty ideas to start you thinking of new financing approaches:

1. Personal savings

The first place to look for business financing is with yourself. Investors and lenders will not risk their money in your business if you're not willing to risk your own money. Outside investors and lenders will likely require you to invest a reasonable amount before they will supplement it.

Savings include your checking accounts, savings accounts, CDs, mutual funds, stocks, bonds, and other liquid assets that you can use to start a business.

If you've done your homework, you know how much you need. You've saved and planned accordingly. If not, it may be best to delay the new business venture until you accumulate sufficient savings. Cut back on personal expenditures. Pay yourself first by saving a reasonable percentage before all other expenditures. Consider working overtime at your current job or moonlighting at a second job to increase your needed savings.

2.   Sale of personal assets

If you don't have sufficient liquid assets, such as savings and investments, consider selling other assets.

Prepare an inventory of all the assets that you own, estimate their value, and determine which ones are expendable. Possibilities include investment real estate or a home that might be larger or more expensive than you need. Also consider automobiles, boats, partnership interests, corporation interests, and other personal property.

Consider holding a garage sale to accumulate additional cash by selling used books, clothing, or furniture. Perhaps you own some valuable collectibles such as antiques, coins, or baseball cards. These could be an additional source of untapped cash.

3.   Home-equity loans

If you own a home, a great source of funds is a home-equity loan. Lenders are more concerned that you have sufficient equity in the property than with how you spend the proceeds. Thus, you won't need to be as persuasive in convincing them of the viability of the enterprise. Consider obtaining a home-equity loan while you are still employed and have a steady income stream, which lenders love.

Home-equity loans have three other benefits. First, the interest rates are lower because sufficient equity in local real estate secures the debt. Second, the loans are often for a substantial time period. Loans of ten, fifteen, and thirty years are possible. Third, the tax law favors home-equity loans. Interest on up to $100,000 of home-equity loans is an itemized deduction, regardless of how you use the proceeds. If you can trace the proceeds into your business, the interest qualifies as business interest, and is 100% deductible on your business schedule or business return. For individuals, this reduces income subject to both income tax and self-employment tax.

4. Personal borrowing

Consider several other borrowing alternatives you have. If you own a whole-life insurance policy with cash value, you can borrow on the cash value at very favorable rates. Check with your insurance agent for the specifics.

You can also obtain cash advances up to your limits on the credit cards. You can make purchases for business supplies and assets on the credit cards. Credit card interest rates are high. Don't use this type of borrowing for long-term purposes. However, it is helpful to have access to the credit lines when needed.

If you have a current job with a stable salary, apply for several credit cards. Request increases of your credit lines on a regular basis. You may never need access to such lines, but they're valuable to have.

Even if you never plan to use the cash-advance credit on your credit cards, they are an excellent means of simplifying your record-keeping chores.

Carry four credit cards for expenditures. Use one card for business supplies, business equipment, business seminars, and all other business items that are 100% business tax deductible. Use a second credit card for business meals and entertainment, that currently have reduced deduction rules. Use a third credit card for automobile expenses, which you must later prorate between business and personal use. Use the fourth credit card for purely personal expenditures.

This method minimizes the number of checks you write, and it is an excellent way to keep organized receipts for year-end record keeping and potential audit documentation. It will make your CPA very happy.

5. Love money

"Love money" is financing that you receive from friends, relatives, and other acquaintances to assist you in starting the business. Think seriously whether you even want to consider such funding. You may be happier strictly separating business and personal relationships. Such requests can put your friends and relatives in a difficult and uncomfortable position. Many close personal relationships have later soured because of bad business or investment experiences.

If you do proceed, ensure that all parties understand the investment specifics. Clarify whether the investment is equity, debt, gift, or any hybrid. Document the agreement with all details in writing.

Ensure that all parties understand the relationship and how you will use the funds. Inform them of all the risks involved. Ensure that the fund providers can financially afford such risks.

The parties should also be aware of their potential liability, especially if they are general partners. Consider classifying the investor as a lender. Alternately, consider using a limited partnership or corporation if liability limitation is an issue.

6. Bank loans

Banks are conservative and unlikely to loan to start-up businesses absent other factors. They may loan to start-ups with an SBA guaranteed loan. They may also loan if you have an existing relationship with them, have equity in real estate, or have other assets to secure a loan.

Establish a solid banking relationship before you really need it. Build a long-term, trusting, open relationship with a banker. Obtain small loans and pay them off early to establish a solid track record.

It's much easier to obtain loans, just as it's much easier to acquire credit cards, while you have a secure, salaried, full-time job. If you are still in that position, take action before you enter into the insecure entrepreneurial world.

Establish a good credit record. Pay your bills on time and don't overextend yourself. Obtain a small loan or buy some items on credit to help establish your credit. Periodically obtain a copy of your credit report, and check it for accuracy.

Your business loan package should contain

- An updated business plan
- Personal financial statements of the owners
- Resumes of the key management people
- Tax returns of the business or owners for the past two years
- Cover letter clarifying
  - Amount requested
  - Purpose of loan

- Term of loan
- Source of repayment
- Collateral
- Alternate repayment methods

7. Finance companies

Finance companies often make loans that banks reject. Finance companies will take a greater risk, but they also charge a higher interest rate to compensate. A finance company should not be your first choice, but if a bank turns you down, it may be a necessary alternative. Talk with several finance companies, just as you talk with several banks, so you can compare services.

8. Small Business Administration (SBA) guaranteed loans

SBA *direct* loans are extinct, but SBA *guaranteed* loans are still available. Commercial banks and other lending agencies process the SBA guaranteed loans. The SBA covers a substantial portion of their risk. The bank is more likely to make the loan because its chance for loss is less.

There are many misconceptions about SBA guaranteed loans. The SBA does not give away anything, and they are not in the business of losing money. Its guarantee puts the government at risk if you don't repay the loan. The SBA verifies that your credit is good and that you have sufficient collateral.

Loan amounts generally range from $50,000 to $750,000. Smaller loan amounts may be available through other government or private programs.

Rates on SBA guaranteed loans are negotiable, but generally range from 2 percent to 3 percent above the prime rate. In addition, the borrower pays the SBA a loan guarantee fee ranging from 3 percent to 3.875 percent of the principal. There are no loan prepayment penalties.

It's not easy to qualify for the guarantee. The interest rate isn't a bargain, but there are benefits. The big plus is actually obtaining the loan in the first place. You also have the chance to stretch payments over a longer period than the two to three years conventional lenders generally allow.

The average term of an SBA loan is nine years, which allows lower monthly payments. Fifteen-year terms are common. For certain real estate transactions, you can extend payments up to twenty-five years. SBA guarantees loans to start-ups and ongoing businesses. Start-ups account for approximately one-third of the loans.

A bank does not need to reject your loan application before you apply. However, a lender has to specify that you could not obtain a loan at a reasonable term without the guarantee. SBA also expects a new business to contribute approximately 30 percent of the capital needed. There are industry size limits on obtaining the loan. Most businesses with fewer than five hundred employees qualify.

The process itself is straightforward. You submit a loan application to a bank or other lender. After reviewing the application, the lender sends it to an SBA loan officer at their closest district office. If it's approved, you receive the proceeds shortly. You repay the lender according to the negotiated terms. Preferred-lender-status and certified-lender-status financial institutions process the paperwork even faster because the SBA delegates more of the decision making to them.

9. SBA 504 program

The SBA 504 program is a loan program designed to enhance community economic development through job creation and retention. The program assists small business with capital investments that include machinery, equipment, and real estate. It provides fixed-asset financing for up to twenty years. Three investors come together in the financial package. There is at least 10 percent owner equity, up to 40 percent SBA guaranteed debt, and 50 percent third-party, private-sector financing. Any real estate must generally be more than 50 percent owner-occupied. The SBA 504 program can make loans up to $1 million.

10. Other government financial programs

Other government financing options are available. Check with federal, state, and local agencies. Financing programs, terms, and requirements change regularly. Contact the government agencies for details. Many have specific lending programs to encourage certain businesses, or to encourage businesses in certain areas. Some have grants available, and some even make equity investments in a company.

Two of the most appropriate state agencies to contact are your state Department of Commerce and your state Department of Economic Development. Check with your state, county, and city for additional agencies and departments available to assist small businesses.

One federal program that entrepreneurs should be aware of is Small Business Innovation Research (SBIR). It started in 1982 and has served as a highly competitive program spurring technological innovation among qualified small businesses. The goal of the program is to meet the needs of eleven federal government agencies.

The SBIR program consists of three phases:

Phase 1: This phase evaluates the value and technical feasibility of a project. An award up to $50,000 for six months of research is available.

Phase 2: This phase encompasses expansion and further development based upon the results obtained in Phase 1. Research and development programs usually have a two-year maximum period. Awards of up to $500,000 are possible.

Phase 3: This is the commercialization stage of a project. SBIR funding stops at this point. You must obtain private non-SBIR financing.

The eleven federal agencies are responsible for selecting topics, issuing solicitations, evaluating proposals, and bestowing awards for the program. The SBA publishes a quarterly listing of presolicitation announcements that contain the basic information concerning SBIR solicitations. For more information and to be added to the mailing list, write to:

U.S. Small Business Administration
OIR & T, Room 500
1441 L Street, NW
Washington, DC 20416

11. Business partners

Think about going into business with a partner. Besides the additional service, advice, and expertise, a business partner can also contribute financially. If you don't have the funds to go it alone, consider combining resources with other like-minded entrepreneurs. It could increase your chance for success.

However, business partnerships have certain disadvantages. Disputes can arise as to how to run the business, and as to who is responsible for what. Make sure you know prospective business partners well before entering into an agreement. Make sure that you have a complete written agreement defining the duties, obligations, and rights of each party.

Find partners with complementary talents, rather than clones of yourself. This increases your chance for success in the business. For example, if you have great financial skills, adding two partners with great financial skills is not optimizing your chance for business success. It would be much more effective to add partners with marketing or operations skills to complement your financial skills.

Seriously consider using the limited partnership or the corporate form of ownership instead of the general partnership. General partners all have say in the management of the business, but they also all have unlimited liability. A limited partnership or a corporation may be more appropriate, even though they are more complex and will probably cost more to form.

12. Angels

Thousands of individual investors contribute seed capital to start-ups when more established sources turn deaf ears. These independent investors are "angels." Because they are unaffiliated with any formal venture capital network, angels are especially hard to identify. It's wise to attend local business meetings and talk with professional contacts. Angels discover most of the companies they invest in through word of mouth. Ask your attorney, accountant, financial planner, and banker for possible contacts.

Angels appear in a variety of forms and have a variety of strategies. Some look for a sure thing. Some want a large share in the equity of the business. Some want to make substantial capital gains quickly. Some want to tell you how to run your business, while others just want to be part of something new and exciting. Some have ceilings on how much they are willing to invest, while others won't invest below a certain amount.

Be prepared and do your homework. Impress the potential investor with your knowledge and experience in the business, and with the potential of the business. Have a formal, written agreement with investors that clearly explains the relationship.

13. Small business investment companies (SBICs)

SBICs make venture and risk investments by supplying equity capital and extending unsecured loans to small enterprises that meet their criteria. They help with straight loans and equity investments, providing management assistance to the companies they finance. Most SBICs concentrate more on later-stage and leveraged buy-out deals, where more companies can afford to mix debt with equity. However, they do provide start-up dollars for new companies as well. Each SBIC seems to have its own specialty.

To obtain a directory of the approximately 200 SBICs across the country licensed by the SBA to invest in small business, write to
National Association of Small Business
Investment Companies (NASBIC)
1156 15th Street NW, Suite 1101
Washington, DC 20005

14. Venture capital

The principal source of financing for high-growth potential companies comes from the venture capital industry. SBICs usually take a debt or a small-equity position. However, venture capitalists usually take only an equity interest, planning for long-term appreciation. By numbers, the SBICs are dominant. By dollars, venture capitalists have provided about 90 percent of venture capital equity investments.

Venture capitalists normally provide capital in return for convertible preferred stock. They're willing to ride out their investment for three to seven years. They don't require any cash return until the company shares become liquid. This usually occurs through an initial public offering or a merger with, or acquisition by, a public corporation.

An entrepreneur seeking this form of capital must provide a comprehensive business plan that describes the entrepreneur's dream. The plan should have a strong, concise executive summary that commands attention. The business plan should include the management team's qualifications. It should include a statement of the capital required and the projected investor pay-back within five years.

Venture capital is not a realistic financing alternative for most start-up businesses. Typically, venture capitalists will look at only ten out of one hundred business plans submitted. They will fund only one or two of these ten plans. You need to have a great idea and a great management team to be a candidate.

The principal reference source in the industry is *Pratt's Guide to Venture Capital Sources*, published by Venture Economics, Inc., of Wellesley Hills, Massachusetts. It is available at most libraries. It lists the names and locations of active capital venture firms and contains some helpful articles. There are also venture capital clubs across the country. A directory of approximately 115 venture capital clubs is available from

International Venture Capital Institute, Inc.
P.O. Box 1333
Stamford, CT 06904

15. Leasing

Leasing, rather than buying, is one of the most popular ways to defer expenditures. Instead of requiring a large outlay of cash to purchase an asset, a lease spreads payments out over time, typically three to five years. You can budget for lease payments, thereby simplifying cash flow planning.

Leasing may be more expensive than buying or borrowing in the long-run, but leasing preserves precious working capital. It also preserves borrowing power by allowing companies to acquire assets without depleting existing credit sources. You report it on financial statements as a footnote entry, thereby providing off-balance-sheet financing that improves key operating ratios. Be sure to calculate the "finance charge" of leasing. It often equates to a 15 percent to 20 percent effective interest rate.

The credit criteria of lease financing companies may be less stringent than those of bank credit companies. Leases are available even in times of tight money, when cash loans may be hard to obtain. Leasing also receives favorable tax treatment and provides the technological advantages of quicker access to productive assets and less risk of obsolescence. This is especially important for rapidly changing technology such as data processing and tele-communications. Many leases provide options to purchase and permit exchanges for more advanced equipment as it becomes available.

16. Customer financing

Why don't you have your customers finance your business? There are a variety of ways to do this.

Large, well-known companies will often finance companies that make products it can sell or that will complete a product line. DuPont Company, for example, has funded dozens of young companies with products in advanced materials, electronic imaging, medical imaging, and biotechnology.

There are several other ways to utilize customer financing. You can *license* your products or ideas for a fee. You can form *joint ventures* with customers. You can *franchise* your business. Franchising allows you to sell the rights to produce or market your product or service to other interested parties. You can sell additional items like *newsletters, seminars*, or *consulting services*.

Give your customers an incentive for paying fast and paying in advance, even if you have to offer additional products or discounts. You want to obtain the money due you as soon as possible. The customer also benefits by obtaining additional products or services or a discount. Make it clearly in the customer's best interest to pay as soon as possible and to pay as much up front as possible.

17. Supplier financing

Some of the same ideas discussed above for customer financing also apply to supplier financing. However, also consider that you are a customer of the supplier. Suppliers want to sell you supplies, inventory, or equipment, so let them be your financing source. Do not pay cash. Negotiate for excellent payment terms, stretching out payments for as long as possible for as low an amount as possible. Request that additional products or services be included with the transaction. Remember, it doesn't hurt to ask. You won't get these benefits unless you ask.

Consider bartering your goods and services. Ask suppliers if they need what you sell. Many industries use barter extensively. It can be a win-win situation for you and your supplier.

18. Factoring accounts receivable

If you don't obtain all your money up front at the time of the sale, you have accounts receivable.

One way to obtain cash for those receivables is to "sell" them to a factor. The factor pays you cash up to a percentage of the receivables value. Customers make their payments to the factor. The factor keeps the full amount, making a profit on the discount. You benefit by obtaining cash early.

Discounts vary. They depend upon the risk assumed by the factor and the age of the receivables. Generally, expect a 5 percent to 20 percent discount on the face value of your receivables.

19. Initial public offering (IPO)

If you have a great idea with a lot of potential, you may obtain financing through an initial public stock offering. However, this is more likely to occur later in your business, after you have established substantial growth and success.

An IPO is an issuance of stock to large numbers of unknown investors. IPOs are expensive and time-consuming. However, they can generate substantial funds for the business. The process can make the founder of the company very wealthy.

Keep it in mind as a future financing opportunity. For most entrepreneurs, it's not an option at the start-up phase.

20. Bootstrap

Bootstrapping may be the best method of all for financing your new business. Bootstrapping involves starting small and conservatively. After becoming successful, you continually plow back the profits into the business, rather than distributing them to the owners.

You may have several great ideas. You may want to go after several different markets and do everything at once. However, a more logical approach suggests starting with one product in one market, making that successful, and then gradually increasing the markets or increasing the products. Take minimum amounts of money out of the business for your own use, and plow the rest back into the business to expand. It will grow exponentially and will likely be the best investment you can make.

Periodically review this list of financing opportunities. An option that was not appropriate in the past may be a great choice sometime later.

CHAPTER **13**
ACTION ITEMS

Determining Financial Needs and Resources

1. List all your projected start-up costs.

2. List all your projected operating costs.

3. Determine and explain your most appropriate financing sources.

CHAPTER 14

Choosing the Right Entity

Lawsuit protection is often a major concern of business owners. Limiting personal liability is one of the most important factors in choosing your form of business entity, but there are many other issues also to consider. Entity choice is one of the first major legal and tax business decisions you will need to make.

The six major entity choices available are

1. Sole proprietorship
2. General partnership
3. Limited partnership
4. Limited liability company or limited liability partnership (in this book, abbreviated LLC for both)
5. C corporation
6. S corporation

In some states and under some conditions, a business might choose to form a joint venture, cooperative, business trust, or syndicate. However, for most businesses, the choice will be one of the six major entities.

This chapter divides the choices into three major categories: (1) sole proprietorships, (2) partnerships (which includes discussion of general partnerships, limited partnerships, and LLCs), and

(3) corporations (which includes discussion of both C and S corporations). The chapter explains the characteristics, major advantages, and major disadvantages of each form. It discusses important elements to consider when forming partnerships or corporations and when drafting the legal documents.

SOLE PROPRIETORSHIPS

A sole proprietorship is the most common form of business ownership. It consists of one individual owner who has not taken steps to incorporate. By default, that entity is a sole proprietorship.

Sole Proprietorship Characteristics

Formation: One individual starts and operates a business with an intent to make a profit. If spouses jointly own and operate a business, it is technically a general partnership. There are minimal formation costs.

Investment: Individual owner has 100 percent equity interest.

Control: Individual owner has 100 percent control.

Duration: It terminates on death or bankruptcy of owner or upon voluntary closure by owner.

Liability: Individual owner has 100 percent personal liability.

Taxation: The owner reports the business net income and pays both income tax and self-employment tax. The owner reports revenues and expenses on Schedule C of the owner's individual income tax return.

Sole Proprietorship Advantages

- Formation is fast and easy with few formalities or legal restrictions.
- Expenses, licensing fees, and filing fees are minimal.
- Owner needs only minimal legal and tax help.
- Owner has complete control.
- Owner is the sole recipient of all the profits.
- Owner can use losses in the business to offset other income on the personal income tax return.
- Owner has relative freedom from government regulations and tax return filing requirements.
- Termination is easy.

Sole Proprietorship Disadvantages

- Owner has unlimited personal liability for business debts.
- Owner has total responsibility for everything.
- Owner's own skills, time, assets, and funds limit chances for success.
- Financing may be difficult to obtain.

PARTNERSHIPS

Partnerships consist of two or more individuals or entities that operate a business with the intent to make a profit. They have not taken the legal steps to become a corporation or an LLC. General partnerships consist of all general partners. Limited partnerships have at least one general and one limited partner. LLCs, which this section also discusses, strive for the liability protection of a corporation and the taxability of a partnership.

Partnership Characteristics

Formation: The oral or written agreement of two or more individuals or entities to operate a business with the intent to make a profit constitutes a general partnership. (A general partnership of limited duration or scope is a *joint venture*. It has the same attributes as a general partnership.) Limited partnerships and LLCs require the filing of a statutory form, and the payment of filing fees to the appropriate state agency, in addition to an agreement.

Investment: General partners and LLC members can contribute cash, property, or services. Limited partners can contribute only cash or property.

Control: Each general partner has an equal say in management unless expressly agreed otherwise. Limited partners have no say in the day-to-day management but may participate in major business decisions. The LLC agreement governs LLC members. It can give management control to members or to a manager.

Duration: The partnership agreement specifies termination events of general and limited partnerships. Agreement by the partners, death, bankruptcy, or withdrawal of a general partner also terminates a partnership. LLCs generally terminate upon agreement of the members.

Liability: General partners have *joint and several* liability for actions of the partnership. They are also liable for actions of the partners related to the partnership business. If they properly form and operate the entity, the limited partners and LLC members have no personal liability. They can lose only the amount of their investment or investment commitment to the entity.

Taxation: The three entities themselves file tax returns but do not pay federal income taxes. The earnings, whether distributed or not, flow through to the partners or members in accordance with the agreement. The partners and members report their share and pay income tax and self-employment tax, if applicable, on their earnings. Each state has its own rules on taxation and fees of the entities.

Partnership Advantages

- Original owner has additional sources of investment capital to start and grow the business.
- Partners have each other to help in decision making.
- Availability of partners may eliminate the need for hiring employees.
- A general partnership is quite easy and inexpensive to start.
- Partners can spread the risk and stabilize the business through sharing and utilization of resources, skills, and experiences.
- General partnerships are relatively free from government control.
- Flow-through of income avoids double taxation.
- Flow-through of losses can offset other personal income.
- Sharing of profits can motivate production.

Partnership Disadvantages

- There is unlimited *joint and several* personal liability for all general partners. Joint and several liability means that the partners can be sued as a group or individually for full satisfaction of an obligation.
- Partners may have disputes and disagreements.
- There may be difficulty in delineating authority, responsibility, and contributions.

- Sharing of profits may cause problems.
- There are substantial governmental filing requirements and fees for limited partnerships and LLCs.
- Partnership requires a separate entity tax return.
- There is more need for legal and tax services.
- Dissolution and termination are more difficult and expensive.

Going into business with someone else is risky. Thoroughly check your colleague's background and credit history. Make sure the chemistry is right and that you share common goals. Clearly establish responsibilities and communicate frequently. Find someone who complements your skills and adds something to the business. Make sure you have a written agreement for your partnership or other legal entity. Hire a good business lawyer to draft or review it.

At a minimum, be sure to consider the following issues in your partnership agreement:

- Name of the partnership
- Purpose of the partnership
- Duration of the partnership
- Business office address
- Names and contributions of each partner
- Additional and future contributions
- Consequences if future contributions are not made
- Sharing of profits and losses
- Allocation of tax items
- Distributions and loans to partners
- Salaries or guaranteed payments to partners
- Fringe benefits
- Duties and responsibilities of each partner
- Policy on hiring family members
- Limitations on outside business activities
- Dispute resolution
- Admission of new partners
- Valuation on dissolution, withdrawal, death, disability, divorce
- Liquidation on dissolution, withdrawal, death, disability

- Buy-sell agreements and life and disability insurance
- Retirement of partner requirements
- Noncompetition clauses for departing partners
- Termination or expulsion of partner provisions
- Accounting and tax decisions and elections
- Banking and check-signing power
- Right of first refusal and transfer limitations
- Contractual power and prohibited acts of partners
- Financial statements and access to records
- Signatures of all parties and spouses

CORPORATIONS

Corporations are separate legal entities owned by one or more shareholders that require filing and payment of fees to a state agency. Corporations are separate taxable entities for federal tax purposes unless they file an S election form with the IRS. The S corporation reports income and expense as a flow-through entity. Owners of the entity report the income and pay the tax.

Corporation Characteristics

Formation: File articles of incorporation with the secretary of state or other applicable office.

Investment: Flexible ownership is available with stock issued for cash, property, or services. Stock can be common or preferred, voting or nonvoting, and have many other variables. S corporation stock has substantial limitations.

Control: Stock shareholders elect a board of directors who set policy and appoint officers to manage the day-to-day activities.

Duration: A corporation has perpetual existence unless dissolved.

Liability: There is no personal liability for shareholders if they properly form and operate the entity. Shareholders can lose only what they invested or committed to invest in the business.

Taxation: A C corporation is a separate taxable entity and pays taxes on its profits at applicable federal and state rates; shareholders pay taxes on dividend distributions, which results in the double taxation problem. S corporations pass through the proportionate share of income to the shareholders, as in a partnership.

Corporation Advantages

- **Choice of state**

The owners may choose the state in which they wish to incorporate. They generally will be subject to the laws and disclosure and reporting rules of that state, and they will pay the applicable fees.

Several states, most notably Delaware and Nevada, pride themselves on being havens for business incorporations. These states have low incorporation fees, probusiness corporate laws, and substantial secrecy afforded to corporate owners. However, a business can't escape state income tax by merely incorporating in a certain state. Any state where the company "does business" or makes sales will tax the income if it has a state income tax.

If you incorporate in one state, but you do all your business in another, you have complicated your life. The state you operate in will tax you and will require you to register to do business in that state. You will also pay additional administrative fees to the state where you incorporated.

Most small businesses that decide to incorporate should consider doing so in the state in which they will be doing most, if not all, of their business. If you conduct activities in several states, or if you make sales in several states, compare the corporation laws and procedures of those states. If you have a business that allows you to choose the sale location, such as mail order, you have more options. Select the most appropriate state to incorporate in, and then structure the business to generate the sales from that state.

- **Contract liability**

Minimizing personal liability is a prime reason to incorporate. Liabilities come in several forms. The corporate veil can limit personal liability on contracts at times. However, it may be impossible to limit it at other times.

Examples of contracts a new business would enter into include bank loans, lease agreements, and employment agreements. On a bank loan, the bank typically requires the owners to sign or guarantee the loan in their individual capacities as well as in the corporate capacity. This requirement prevents owners from limiting personal liability. If the corporation defaults on the loan, the owners are personally liable.

In the case of employment contracts and most supplier and customer contracts, it is unlikely that the owners will have to sign personally. If there is a breach of contract, the corporation will be liable. The corporate veil will normally shield the individual owners from personal liability.

Leases are good examples of contracts that could go either way. In some cases, landlords require shareholders to sign personally. In other cases, they do not. It all depends on the facts and circumstances. Never volunteer to assume personal liability. If they ask you to sign a lease personally, consider the alternatives. Depending on the current rental market and your negotiating ability, you may be able to avoid signing personally if you insist on it, and the landlord strongly wants you as a tenant. Don't be afraid to walk away from the deal.

- **Tort liability**

Examples of tort liability are personal injury claims and product liability claims. Generally, if a corporate employee commits a tort, the corporation is liable and that employee is liable. However, the individual shareholders are not personally liable. Thus, a corporation is usually good protection against personal liability on such claims.

- **Professional liability**

State corporate law now allows most professionals to incorporate. However, they generally can't shield themselves from personal liability for their own professional malpractice. For example, if an individual doctor incorporates and later commits malpractice, then both the corporation and the individual doctor are liable to the claimant. Thus, forming a professional corporation is not a shield against your own personal professional malpractice.

However, if several professionals go into business together, a corporation is still appropriate. If they form a general partnership, and one professional partner commits malpractice, then all the professional partners have personal liability. However, if a shareholder of a professional corporation commits malpractice, only the corporation and that particular shareholder are liable. The other shareholders are not personally liable.

- **Multiple owners**

With more than one owner of a business, the entity choices are partnership, corporation, and LLC. Partnerships have their disadvantages, but they do work best when there are only a few general partners. A general partnership becomes unwieldy with too many owners. With more people involved, a corporation, or perhaps an LLC, becomes a much more viable entity. Major public corporations have millions of shareholders, and they are still able to operate efficiently. A large general partnership is much more difficult to manage, since all general partners have say in the day-to-day management. If the owners of a family business wish to divide the ownership of the business into various "pieces," the corporation or LLC is a much more efficient vehicle than a partnership.

• **Streamlined administration**

Over the years, corporate management has developed into an efficient system with a long history of operating rules and traditions. Shareholders are the owners of the corporation, and they elect a board of directors to make the major management decisions of the corporation. The board of directors then elects officers to manage the business on a day-to-day basis. The officers then hire employees to work in the corporation. Thus, even corporations with many shareholders operate and run efficiently. Partnerships are not as streamlined.

• **Perpetual existence**

A corporation never dies. Shareholders of the corporation may die. They may pass on their shares to their heirs. However, the corporation itself remains in existence until the shareholders take some action to dissolve it. The state may also take action if the corporation does not pay the fees and taxes. Partnerships, on the other hand, often will terminate upon the death, disability, or insolvency of a partner.

• **Voting and the value division.**

Shareholders are the owners of the corporation's stock. In many cases, the corporation issues only one class of stock. However, it is possible to issue many varieties of stock to appropriately divide original issue value, voting rights, dividend rights, liquidation rights, and so on. This provides for an infinite variety of tax, business, and estate planning techniques that allow the owners of the corporation to achieve their goals, accept the risks, and obtain the benefits they desire. Remember, however, that an S corporation may issue only one class of stock.

- **Stock versus debt**

Should you take stock or debt in exchange for your cash or property contributions? Stock has the advantage of ownership and potential appreciation. Debt has the advantage of regular payments of interest and the future return of the principal without adverse tax consequences. The owners must ensure that the corporation has sufficient stock investment to have economic substance, and that it is not a sham for tax or liability purposes.

- **Forced formality**

Some sole proprietorships seem to blend in with the owner's personal life, from both management and financial standpoints. However, a corporation is a separate entity. Corporations require separate books and records. Corporations hold annual meetings to make or confirm corporate decisions. If shareholders don't take proper steps and don't comply with formalities, they risk piercing the *corporate veil* for both tax and liability purposes. Impress upon the corporate owners the importance of keeping separate books and records and of setting up and adequately funding the corporation. Ensure that they issue stock properly and have at least one annual meeting of shareholders and the board of directors. Stress the need to always sign corporate documents and contracts in the corporate capacity.

- **Prestige**

Some believe that a business operating as a corporation is more prestigious than a business operating as a sole proprietorship or partnership. Many automatically assume that a corporation is a larger and more financially secure operation than a sole proprietorship or partnership. This may not be fair, but it is a common misperception.

It also may be important for the business to be a corporation in certain industries, if a business's competitors are corporations. Being able to call yourself "chair of the board" and "president," even if the corporation has only one shareholder and one employee, might enhance your prestige.

- **Name protection**

Protecting the name of a business can be a complex issue. Name protection involves common and statutory law, as well as both federal and state law. However, there is some protective value in incorporating under a particular name.

A state will not allow you to incorporate under a name that is exactly the same as an already existing corporation in that state, or under a deceptively similar name. If you incorporate under a certain name, you do have certain rights. You may be able to prevent others from incorporating under the same, or a deceptively similar, name in your state in the future. However, if name protection is of substantial importance, consult a trademark attorney for added protection. Merely being given the permission to incorporate under a certain name does not guarantee you the right to use that name in your particular trade or business or in your particular area.

- **Decreased audit potential**

The Internal Revenue Service (IRS) rarely audits small corporations. The IRS is more likely to audit an individual with Schedule C sole proprietorship income. This is not necessarily fair, but it is a fact drawn from audit statistics. The IRS audits large corporations frequently, but small corporations seem to escape audit scrutiny.

There is also a potential bias found in some auditors. When looking at a Schedule C on an individual's return, auditors often assume there are personal expenses listed on that Schedule C. It is now their job to find them. More often, the mind-set when auditing a corporate return is that the corporation is a separate business entity, and there is less chance of finding personal expenditures in the tax return. This is unfair, but it is a factor to consider.

- **15% federal tax rate**

Regular C corporations that are not *personal service corporations,* pay taxes of 15 percent on the first $50,000 of taxable income. This is the lowest rate in recent corporate tax history. An individual with a sole proprietorship, whether that individual is single or married, would likely have this income taxed in the 28 percent, 31 percent, 36 percent, or 39.6 percent federal tax bracket. For many small businesses, the ability to have $50,000 taxed in a 15 percent bracket is a good tax planning opportunity.

- **Double-pocket theory**

In a corporation (other than an S corporation) there are two entities—the corporation and the individual owner—that you can use to obtain the best total economic and tax benefits. There must be economic substance behind each decision. However, legitimate tax planning can move income between the two entities. For example, if the corporation is having a poor year, lower the salaries and dividends. Likewise, if the individual owner is in a low tax bracket this year, increase salaries from the corporation. You have two taxpayers who have different tax rates and different circumstances each year. The desired end result is maximization of the total benefits to the owner, and minimization of the total tax.

- **Loans from retirement plans**

Generally, the rules on pension and profit-sharing plan contributions are the same for corporations, partnerships, and sole proprietorships. However, there is one remaining benefit for corporate plan participants. If the plan permits, within certain dollar limits, corporate plan participants may be able to obtain loans from their pension or profit-sharing plans. This can be a good source of cash if needed. However, it is important to properly document the loan, make payments regularly, and not exceed the loan amount legal limits.

- **Health insurance**

One major advantage of a C corporation over other entity forms is the many fringe benefits. The corporation pays and deducts these for the benefit of the employees. The individual owner does not pay tax on the benefits. Perhaps the premier fringe benefit that this applies to is health insurance. Individuals can incorporate the business and hire themselves as employees. They can then set up a health insurance plan for the employees and make deductible payments to the health insurance provider. The business owner is paying health insurance with *before-tax* dollars rather than with *after-tax* dollars.

- **Group term life insurance**

Group term life insurance is another fringe benefit that is much more useful for C corporations than other entities. Up to $50,000 face value of group term life insurance per employee can be paid and deducted by a corporation as a business expense. The employee pays no tax on the benefit. Upon the death of the employee, the insurance company pays the proceeds to the beneficiary with no income tax consequences.

- **Medical reimbursement plan**

A C corporation can also set up a medical reimbursement plan. Corporations often use this plan in addition to health insurance.

The reimbursement plan often covers the deductible portion of medical expenses, the co-insurance portion of medical expenses, and perhaps other uninsured medical expenses. Only the C corporation can deduct these expenditures for employees while still allowing the employee to avoid the taxability of the benefit.

- **Disability insurance**

Disability insurance is a fourth fringe benefit that is more beneficial to C corporations. Disability insurance pays a portion of the lost income of an employee who becomes disabled, whether or not that disability occurs on the job. The corporation can pay and deduct premiums on an individual employee's disability policy. The current benefit of being covered by such disability insurance is not taxable to the individual. This fringe benefit is better than most from the owner's viewpoint. The owner can discriminate and cover only certain key employees instead of all employees.

- **Other fringe benefits**

There are additional fringe benefits from which a C corporation receives better tax treatment than other entity forms. These include employee death benefits, deferred compensation, split-dollar life insurance, and cafeteria plans. Cafeteria plans provide employees with a menu of benefits to choose from.

- **Stock options**

Stock options allow individuals the choice at a future date to purchase shares of stock of the corporation at a set price. Because only corporations issue stock, this feature is unique to corporations. Other entities can't offer stock options (although LLCs may have similar features). A variety of stock options are available. Some have better tax benefits than others. The major use of a stock option is as a "carrot" for key employees, which enables corporations to pay less in current compensation and benefits. Stock options serve as incentives for key management and marketing personnel. If they have confidence in the company, and if the company does well (often because of the work that they have put in), they receive rewards. They will be able to buy stock at a bargain price in the future. The benefits to the company are the increased value of the stock, elimination of current cash outlay, and the payment of future benefits in equity of the company rather than in cash.

- **Fiscal year**

Corporations need to elect an accounting period for tax purposes. S corporations *and personal service corporations* must generally use a calendar year. *Nonpersonal service* C corporations can elect a fiscal year without limitation. The factors to consider in choosing a fiscal year might be tax planning, natural business year, or convenience of the owners. The accountant of the corporation may even suggest a fiscal year so that the corporate year-end and the tax return deadline arrive at a less hectic time.

- **S corporation election**

An S corporation can be the best of both worlds. It has the limited liability protection of a corporation and the pass-through tax attributes of a partnership. However, only certain corporations qualify as S corporations. The entity must avoid involuntary termination. The shareholder-employees of the S corporation are under the same fringe benefit rules as partners in a partnership. They do not obtain the preferred fringe benefit treatment of the C corporation.

Generally the rules for S corporation eligibility are as follows:

- There are no more than seventy-five shareholders. (Spouses count as one.)
- Each shareholder must be an individual, estate, small business trust, qualified trust, or tax-exempt organization.
- There are no corporations or partnerships as shareholders.
- There are no nonresident aliens as shareholders.
- The corporation must be domestic (United States).
- The corporation may be a parent of an affiliated group.
- The corporation may have a subsidiary.
- The corporation must have only one class of stock. Voting and nonvoting stock within that class is permissible.
- The corporation cannot represent corporate debt as a second class of stock.

- The corporation must make the election, and all shareholders and other persons who have an interest in the stock must consent.
- The corporation must make the election by the fifteenth day of the third month of the taxable year to be effective for that year.
- The corporation must make any revocation, and a majority of shareholders must consent.
- Acquisition of stock by noneligible shareholders, or too many shareholders, terminates the election immediately.
- Cessation as a "small business" corporation terminates the election immediately.
- The corporation can't make a new election for five years following termination. Relief for inadvertent termination may be available.

If a corporation expects losses in the early years, consider an S election. If the corporation will make income erratically, making planning difficult, consider an S election. If the corporate shareholders don't need fringe benefits and want the simplicity of all income passing through and being taxed once, consider an S election. Also consider it for a corporation that cannot justify compensation to the key employee owners as *reasonable* and deductible under IRS rules.

- **Dividends received deduction**

A corporation can take a special deduction from gross income for dividends received from a domestic corporation that is subject to income tax. Currently, this deduction is

- 70% of dividends received from corporations owned less than 20% by the recipient corporation
- 80% of dividends received from a "20% owned corporation"
- 100% of qualifying dividends received from members of the same affiliated group

This suggests an incentive for a corporation to invest its excess cash reserves in dividend-paying common stocks rather than in the traditional interest-paying obligations.

Corporation Disadvantages

- Federal securities law compliance

Corporations issue stock and bonds, both of which are securities. Issuance of securities requires compliance with federal securities laws or exemption from the registration requirements.

- State securities law compliance

Corporations issuing stock and bonds to residents of any state must also ensure their compliance with the applicable state securities law of that jurisdiction.

- Federal tax rates

An advantage of a corporation is the 15 percent federal tax rate on the first $50,000. However, above that amount, the federal tax rate increases to a point at which the top corporate tax rate is very close to the top individual tax rate.

Federal corporate tax rates are

- 25% on taxable income between $50,000 and $75,000
- 34% on taxable income between $75,000 and $100,000
- 39% on taxable income between $100,000 and $335,000
- 34% on taxable income between $335,000 and $10,000,000
- 35% and 38% rates on income above $10,000,000

- Costs, fees, and expenses

The costs for obtaining proper advice and services in forming the corporation, and for the administrative activities after the corporate formation such as meetings and tax returns, can be substantial.

- Formalities

Corporations require that the participants comply with certain formalities if they want to obtain the corporate benefits. These formalities include

- Setting up and maintaining separate books and records

- – Always signing in a corporate capacity
- – Filing separate corporate tax returns
- – Holding annual meetings of shareholders and directors

- **Double taxation and liquidation issues**

Regular C corporations are subject to corporate tax on taxable income. If the corporation distributes earnings to shareholders as dividends, IRS taxes such income twice. Both the corporation and the shareholder pay tax on it. There is also potential double taxation if the corporation distributes appreciated assets upon liquidation.

- **Net operating loss (NOL) limits**

Regular C corporations that have a net operating loss cannot use the loss unless they have earnings in the three prior years or until they earn taxable income at a later date. Thus, in the early years, they may not be able to use the loss for tax benefits. An S corporation election can eliminate this disadvantage.

- **Accumulated earnings tax and personal holding company tax**

Add these two additional taxes to the regular corporate federal income tax. They apply only to certain corporations. The accumulated earnings tax applies to *earnings and profits* (generally *retained earnings*) over and above certain amounts that the corporation does not distribute to shareholders as dividends. The personal holding company tax is a tax on certain *portfolio* or *personal service* income, which applies to certain closely held corporations.

- **Alternative minimum tax**

Corporations, as well as individuals, are subject to alternative minimum tax. However, one major distinction is that a corporation must make an adjustment for *adjusted current earnings*. This is generally the amount by which its income for accounting purposes exceeds its taxable income. Seventy-five percent of such an amount is an adjustment and may substantially increase total corporate tax.

- **State minimum tax**

Some states have minimum corporate or franchise taxes that they apply whether or not the corporation has taxable income.

California is an example of a state that has a minimum tax of $800 ($600 for the first year for certain qualifying corporations) payable by all corporations regardless of taxable income.

Every business is different. The owner, in consultation with legal and tax advisors, should make the entity decision. Visualize the advantages and disadvantages on a balance scale, and decide in your particular situation which side outweighs the other. Review the advantages and disadvantages, factor in your personal situation, and make an informed decision.

CHAPTER 14
ACTION ITEMS

Choosing the Right Entity

1. Determine the most appropriate entity form for your business, and explain your rationale.

2. List at least five provisions you would want in a partnership agreement.

3. List the major benefits a corporation would provide you.

CHAPTER 15

Location and Lease Choices

Location, location, location. The three most important factors in purchasing real estate may also apply to business, at least with a retail business. However, no matter what type business you start, analyze your location choice carefully. If you choose the wrong location or a bad location, it is expensive and time-consuming to correct. A poor location can cause your business to fail.

This chapter discusses the three concerns you deal with when choosing a location. The first section explains the general geographic location factors. The second section analyzes specific physical location characteristics. The third section discusses lease negotiations and concerns.

GEOGRAPHICAL FACTORS

Think about your ideal geographic location. You would probably want it close to you, your employees, your suppliers, and your customers. You might be able to have it all, but there will likely be some compromises. Which is the most important factor? It may differ with your type of business. Manufacturers may find it most important to be near suppliers or a good supply of employees. Locating near their target market base usually best serves retail and service businesses. If the customer doesn't need to visit you, perhaps your own convenience is most important.

Analyze your needs carefully. If you stress customer service and have a marketing orientation, you make business decisions with what is best for your customer in mind. Most start-up businesses should return to the target market research done earlier.

Know as much as you can about your target market. Know the shopping habits of those customers and the typical market trade area you expect to cover. Besides the library research sources discussed previously, consider information, statistical data, trends, projections, and maps. These are often available from real estate firms, banks, chambers of commerce, newspapers and other media, state and local government agencies, and shopping centers.

Here are some of the key criteria to consider:

Population

Determine if the key demographic characteristics of your target market suggest certain locations. Specific ethnic, religious, and national origin characteristics of your target market clearly indicate certain preferred locations. Income, vocational, and age characteristics might do the same. Also consider the mobility needs and abilities of the market. How far will people travel? What transportation is available?

If appropriate for your decision, research and obtain the following data for any prospective location:

- How many persons or families are in the trading area, and how has this changed over time? Is the area growing or declining?
- What are the demographics of the population? Consider earnings, age, family status, home ownership, and so forth.
- What is the value of homes? What is the average monthly rent? How many prospects own a car? How many prospects own two cars?
- The trading area includes how many businesses? What types of businesses? Will they attract potential customers to you?

Market trends

Evaluate the potential location from a broader, futuristic perspective. What will it be like to do business there in the future? Try to discover and uncover trends. Read local and neighborhood newspapers. Talk with other business owners in the area. Talk with community planning and development departments. Meet with commercial real estate brokers. Seek information from local business and community groups.

Pay specific attention to population shifts, progressiveness of the community, distribution of wealth, new construction, and the community business base. Find out the history of the site. Analyze why former occupants are no longer there.

Competition

Who is your competition? Do you want to be close to them or far away? What are the strong and weak points of your competition? Is it important to have an anchor store to draw business? You need to answer these questions when assessing your location alternatives.

Carefully analyze who is your true competition. If you own a bowling alley, is your competition other bowling alleys, or does it include movie theaters, pool halls, and golf courses? In many businesses, such indirect competition may be more important to analyze than the direct competition.

Don't assume that you want to be far away from your competitors. Analyze your industry and think like a customer. Some businesses, like the local convenience store and the discount warehouse, prefer the competition to be as far away as possible. However, many businesses thrive on having direct or indirect competitors close. Car dealers often congregate together because buyers prefer to shop around for a car. Fast-food stores often group together so that people have a choice and can alternate daily or weekly choices. Consider the thought process of your customer. Don't jump to hasty conclusions on this subject.

Shop the competition. Pretend you are a customer. Ask questions, collect literature, and analyze the strong and weak points of each. How can you best position your business so that, in the mind of the customer, you are not in competition? If you have a powerful and compelling *unique selling proposition*, as discussed in chapter 5, you are offering something the competitors don't have, or something that you perform better.

State and local laws

Be sure to analyze the state and local laws and regulations that apply to your business. Do you need special licenses for your business? States and localities vary tremendously on requirements and on the business types they encourage or discourage.

Consider the laws, rules, regulations, and policies on

- General business licenses
- Specific profession and occupation licenses
- Income, sales, property, and excise taxes
- Liquor and food
- Zoning, traffic, parking, signage, and day or hour restrictions
- Fire, police, and occupational safety requirements

Traffic and accessibility

Depending on the business, this may or may not be a major concern. Certainly, for most retail businesses, traffic and accessibility are crucial. Obtain data on foot and vehicle traffic flow from your state or local transportation agency. Take some time to observe the traffic yourself during various days and times. Study the flow of traffic and the ease of entry to your business.

Consider the availability and cost of public transportation and parking. Check the amount of traffic congestion and the side of the street (sunny, shady, going to work, going home). Analyze the ease of entry and exit, the part of the block, and the neighboring businesses.

PHYSICAL FACTORS

After you determine your general geographic location choice, next analyze specific buildings or addresses within the preferred area. List the important physical factors to consider, and chart your findings on each prospective site.

Here are some potential items to consider

- Age of building
- Condition of building
- Image of building
- Maintenance of building
- Condition and adequacy of all mechanical systems
- Adequacy for electrical and plumbing needs

- Need for remodeling and projected cost
- Size of space and doors
- Adequacy of layout
- Availability of public restrooms
- Availability of storage or warehouse space
- Potential safety hazards
- Building and neighborhood security and lighting
- Adequacy of parking for customers and employees
- Signage limitations
- Compatibility of neighboring businesses
- Convenience for supplier deliveries
- Ability to accommodate future business growth

COMMERCIAL LEASE CONSIDERATIONS

The lease of your premises may be one of the first important contracts you negotiate and sign. It is a major financial undertaking that will often cover many years. Take the time to read and analyze the lease. List and prioritize your concerns to effectively counteroffer and negotiate the final terms. You will likely want to hire an attorney to assist in some or all of these steps.

A lease is an interesting and complex legal document. The landlord or the landlord's attorney drafts the lease strictly from the landlord's viewpoint. Most provisions overwhelmingly benefit and protect the landlord. You are making a mistake if you sign it without negotiating for some changes. Realistic landlords expect to compromise on some issues, but if you don't ask, you won't obtain any changes. Of course, your negotiating power and success depend on a variety of factors. These include the rental market, the vacancy rate in the building, and the personality and power of the negotiating parties.

Read the lease thoroughly, and make a list of all the provisions you would like changed, deleted, or added. Prioritize your most important desires. Discuss strategy and write a letter to the landlord itemizing your requests. Assess the response, review and revise the strategy, and then start negotiating. Remember, as in all negotiations, the party who wants the contract the most will probably lose in the negotiations. If you have other options, and if you are not afraid to walk away from this lease, you will negotiate a better agreement.

Here are some common lease provisions to consider in your negotiations. Suggested changes to make the lease fairer to you are mentioned. Notice that many of the provisions overwhelmingly favor the landlord. You would like them to overwhelmingly favor the tenant, and you can certainly request that. However, realize that there is also a middle ground that is probably fairer for both. Be willing to compromise.

Use of premises

Make this provision as broad as possible. Your first choice is "any business," or "any legal business." However, the landlord will probably want to limit this. Think on a long-term basis. Do not limit yourself to your current activities. Things change and you want the flexibility to change or add activities. Don't assume that the landlord will accept what you might like to do in the future if this provision is not clear. The landlord may decide to charge additional rent for the later privilege, or there may be other tenants in the building or center who will challenge the new use as competitive. Do your best to obtain a broadly worded use provision. Then add "and other related uses" to the end. Insist on a provision stating the landlord will not be unreasonable in consenting to a change in use.

Term and termination

The ideal lease is a series of short-term leases with infinite options to renew. Benefits of a short-term lease are the ability to end the agreement if your needs change, and the ability to renegotiate future terms. Benefits of a long-term lease are that the terms and rates are stable or predictable for that time period. You will have to determine which best meets your needs. Be careful when committing for a long time in a start-up business. There are many things that could change. Think about possible scenarios that would cause you to want to terminate the lease. Consider proposing such events as conditions that would legally allow you to terminate the lease early.

Possibilities include

• Substantial damage to the premises
• Sales dropping below a certain amount
• Going out of business
• Moving

- Death or disability
- Low occupancy
- Increased competition

Be clear on the starting date of the lease and the obligation to pay. Negotiate some compensation for any costs, damages, and lost profits if the building is not ready for your occupancy on the promised date.

Tenant obligations and limitations

Review all your obligations in the lease. See if you can eliminate them or at least reduce the severity of them. Consider forming a corporation, and insist on signing the lease only as a corporate officer, not individually. Refuse to have your spouse or others sign as co-owners or guarantors unless absolutely necessary. Consider a liquidated damages clause for breach. This provision allows you to pay a certain dollar amount, in addition to being current on all obligations, to terminate the lease early with no future liability.

Rent calculation

Make sure you understand whether the landlord calculates rent on the basis of "Useable square feet" or "rentable square feet." *Useable* refers to the area you can physically use in your location, whereas *rentable* includes additional pro-rata amounts of common area. Be sure to consider this when comparing one property with another. Measure the space yourself to be sure the landlord calculated accurately. Check whether you will be paying a flat rate, a percentage of sales, or the higher of the two. Analyze any cost of living adjustment (COLA) formula increases in the rent. Review what the increases would be if the adjustment index had been in effect in prior years.

Free or reduced rent

Know what the market is offering for free or reduced rent. Know what other tenants in the building have received. Try to obtain as much free rent up front as you can, but be willing to accept it later if necessary. If you can't negotiate free rent, consider a reduction in the rate for several months.

Security deposit and prepaid rent

You would like not to have to pay a security deposit or prepaid rent. You will likely have to pay your rent in advance for the upcoming month, but there is no use in paying for the last month of the lease unless you have no other choice. Possible compromises include asking for interest on the security deposit and any prepaid rent, or requesting that it be applied to a future rent payment after a reasonable number of months.

Late payment, interest, grace period

You want to minimize late payment charges and interest, but you don't want to emphasize this point too much. If it's not included in the lease, certainly don't mention it. Try to obtain a grace period of at least five days before rent is delinquent. Keep the interest rate at 10 percent or lower, and the late payment charge at 6 percent or lower.

Options to renew and buy

Obtain as many options to renew the lease as you can, even if the projected rent is substantially higher than you can imagine paying. You can always renegotiate at a later date, but you want to maintain the ability to stay in the location if business is going well. Without an option to renew, the landlord can refuse to re-lease the property to you, or can make an unreasonable offer to re-lease. Try to obtain at least two options to renew for the same length as the original lease. Keep the future rate as low as possible. Request an option to buy the building if you lease the entire building or a large portion of it.

Tenant improvement allowance

When moving into a new or rehabilitated building or space, you may have to make substantial improvements to make it fit to occupy. Such items might include walls, partitions, lighting, electrical, plumbing, ceiling, carpeting, glass, painting, and signs. Generally, the landlord budgets a certain amount to cover these items but waits to determine exactly what type tenant will occupy the premises before constructing the improvements. The landlord often reimburses the tenant a certain dollar amount per square foot to cover all or part of the improvements and contracts for them. Make sure you understand what the allowance covers, and what the landlord expects to provide. Negotiate for a high allowance and prompt payment.

Taxes, insurance, utilities, and maintenance

Understand which party will pay for these expenses in the lease. Often the pro-rata cost will be *passed through* to the tenant by the landlord. Consider putting a dollar or percentage limit on these expenses. Maintain the right to review and audit the bills and records. Check to see if the landlord separately meters utilities. Review the constraints on the landlord's discretionary expenses. Insist that any real estate tax increases caused by a change in ownership not be passed through to you.

Fixtures, alterations, and repairs

Review the definition of fixtures, alterations, and repairs in the lease. Clarify who has payment responsibility. Try to avoid having to obtain permission for *normal* or *regular* expenses you expect to incur. Clearly define any *trade fixtures* that you plan to remove and retain after the lease terminates.

Assignment and sublease

You want to maintain the ability to assign the rights and obligations of your lease or to sublet the premises to another whenever you choose. The landlord almost always wants to prohibit this or allow it only with express permission in writing and often with an additional fee. A good compromise is that the landlord cannot withhold consent without reasonable cause. Define reasonable cause to be a major change in use, or acceptance of a new tenant who doesn't measure up to your credit level.

Parking and common areas

Assess and evaluate the parking availability and access for you, your employees, and your customers. Consider asking for reserved, covered, free, secured, or validated parking. Determine what common areas are available for your use. Restrooms, storage rooms, conference rooms, break rooms, libraries, waiting rooms, lunchrooms, athletic facilities, and locker rooms are some to consider.

Signs and advertising

Think about the signage and any advertising that you plan, and determine whether the lease permits it. Consider the rules and regulations on building, street, lobby, front door, window, and outdoor signs. Check the limitations on color, size, and content.

Arbitration and attorney fees

Consider binding arbitration clauses that require the parties to handle disputes privately with third-party arbitrators, rather than forcing litigation. Attorneys' fee provisions allow a prevailing party to recover damages plus reimbursement of their own attorney fees. Make sure it covers attorneys' fees in arbitration. Limit it to *reasonable* attorneys' fees.

Limiting competition

Is it important to you to avoid competition in the building or center? If so, ask for a provision that prevents the landlord from renting to competitors. Carefully define what a competitor is. If you can't get a limitation or restriction on the whole building or center, consider a limitation within a certain distance from your business.

Insurance and indemnification

The lease likely requires the tenant to have liability insurance of at least $1 million. Research the cost, and consider asking for a reduction in the amount needed. The typical indemnification provision states that the tenant will indemnify the landlord for intentional or negligent acts of the tenant or its agents. Insist on a reciprocal provision indemnifying the tenant for such acts of the landlord or the landlord's agents.

Relocation, expansion, and right of first refusal

If the landlord reserves the right to relocate the tenant at the landlord's discretion, try to eliminate this provision in its entirety. If that's impossible, obtain a reasonable notice provision, an assurance of moving to as good or better location, and payment of all direct and indirect moving costs by the landlord. Try to obtain rights to expand into available adjoining space if needed, and the right of first refusal if vacancies become available in adjoining, larger, or better spaces.

CHAPTER 15
ACTION ITEMS

Location and Lease Choices

1. Describe the most important geographical factors for you to consider in choosing a location.

2. Describe the most important physical factors for you to consider in choosing a location.

3. Describe the most important commercial lease provisions for you to negotiate with a landlord.

Chapter 16

Legal Start-up Issues

Protecting the business name and creations is an important concern for many entrepreneurs. There are a variety of other legal issues to consider in starting and running a business. Chapter 14 covered entity choice decisions, and chapter 15 covered lease negotiations. Chapter 17 covers employment law. This chapter concentrates on start-up, intellectual property, and other miscellaneous legal issues that might arise.

Place business legal issues in the proper context. It is important to understand and handle them. It is important to have the assistance of an experienced and accessible business law attorney. However, handling all the legal areas properly does not ensure business prosperity. Successful marketing is still the key. Nevertheless, comply with all laws. Protect your business from costly litigation and large losses. Keep current on rules and regulations affecting business and your specific industry.

Licenses and taxes

Most start-up legal questions involve licenses and taxes. Carefully study the specific rules for your state and locality. Here are some general guidelines to consider:

Business licenses

Most cities and counties require businesses operating within their jurisdiction to obtain a business license or certificate. They often require this revenue generator whether you have a product or service business, and whether you operate full-time or part-time. They often require it whether you operate in a commercial location or out of your home, and whether or not you have employees. There may be a minimum number of business days' requirement. Check your local rules. Comply with the law, and avoid possible penalties.

Home occupation permits

Businesses operating out of the home are popular, and certainly keep overhead expenses lower. Generally, however, businesses can't legally operate in residential zones. If you plan to operate out of your home, carefully check the local laws to make sure your business qualifies. Also check any condominium, apartment, or homeowner restrictions. Be considerate of all the neighbors who might decide to complain.

Many communities have strict rules to limit home businesses. They won't grant permission if the business substantially increases noise, traffic, lighting, or odors. They usually don't allow businesses that store inventory, handle food, employ workers, or have customer traffic and parking. If granted a permit, you often have strict rules governing storage, signage, and business activities. Consider using a mailbox suite or an executive suite for your business address and deliveries if you cannot justify a full commercial location.

Occupational and professional licenses

Besides the regular business license that all businesses need, certain occupations and most professions require the practitioner to obtain a specific occupation or professional license. The state usually makes and enforces these rules, but there are also some federal licensing requirements. Doctors, lawyers, contractors, and architects are obvious and traditional professions that require licensing. There are many more that are not obvious. Make sure you clearly know the licensing requirements for your occupation or profession. Check with state agencies or others in the same industry. Contracts performed without a required license are generally unenforceable.

Special licenses

Besides the regular business license and the occupational or professional license, certain businesses also need to comply with state or local regulation and licensing requirements. The handling and sale of food and alcohol are highly regulated. These activities have special limitations and regular inspections. Importing and exporting activities may require special licenses.

Local police departments often require certain businesses to obtain special permits to operate. Businesses commonly covered include

- Door-to-door solicitors
- Push-cart vendors
- Entertainment facilities
- Gambling establishments
- Health practitioners
- Massage parlors
- Pawn shops
- Swap meets
- Firearms dealers

Check with your local police department for specific coverage rules.

Fictitious business names

Most businesses use a name, such as Executive Dry Cleaning or Main Street Music, that the owners determine. A fictitious business name is any name that is different from the name of the individual, partnership, or corporate name of the business owners. Any business name that includes the name of the business owner and suggests the existence of additional owners, such as Smith & Company or Jones & Sons, is also a fictitious business name.

Each state has its own rules that you need to research. The California rules are fairly typical and will be used here for illustration only. In California, a business using a fictitious business name must register the name within forty days of starting business. A business that doesn't register its fictitious name cannot use the courts to bring a lawsuit. Banks usually won't open accounts in the fictitious name without registration proof.

In California, you file fictitious business name statements with the county clerk of the business's principal location. Businesses that have no place of business in the state, or that do business in many counties, can file with the clerk's office in Sacramento County.

The fictitious business statement must include

- The fictitious business name
- The street address of the primary place of business
- What form of business it is
- The date the business began doing business using the name
- The signatures of the business owners

Within thirty days of filing the statement, the owners must publish it in a newspaper of general circulation. The paper must be in the California county that is the principal place of business, or in Sacramento County if there is no place of business in California. The statement must run at least once a week for four successive weeks. Within thirty days of completing publication, the owners must file an affidavit (a sworn statement that they published the business statement), including the publication itself, with the county clerk.

California fictitious business name statements expire after five years. You must file again at expiration or within forty days after expiration to renew. Additionally, you must file a new statement within forty days after any required information in the old statement changes.

Resale permits

If you sell products or services on which your state or locality assesses a sales or use tax, you need to obtain a resale permit. Check your specific state requirements. In California, for example, you obtain this permit from the State Board of Equalization. The resale permit allows you to purchase items you will be reselling without paying any sales tax. It also requires you to collect the tax from customers and to remit the tax to the state agency on a regular basis. The agency requires a security bond up front if they believe your sales will be substantial. Be very conservative with your estimate.

INTELLECTUAL PROPERTY

Intellectual property includes trademarks, copyrights, patents, and trade secrets. Applicable federal and state laws balance your right to protect intellectual creations with the free-enterprise, competitive business environment. Consult an attorney who specializes in this area early on so that you can obtain the necessary available protection.

Trademarks and Service Marks

A trademark is a word, phrase, logo or other graphic that a business uses to distinguish its products from those of its competitors. Big Mac™ hamburgers and Kodak™ cameras are examples. A service mark is a name or logo that identifies a service. McDonald's^{SM} restaurants and U-Haul^{SM} truck rental services are examples. In practice, legal protections for trademarks and service marks are identical. Trademark is the term often used for both. The symbol™ indicates you claim a trademark. The symbol ^{SM} indicates you claim a service mark. The symbol ® indicates you have received federal trademark or service mark protection.

The value of a trademark lies in its ability to distinguish the products of the company, and so to attract customers. Generally, the first business to use a protectable mark has the exclusive right to continue using it in the particular locale. That business can sue others to prevent them from using it and any name or graphic similar enough to cause customer confusion.

Not all names receive trademark protection. Ordinary words in their usual context, called *weak* marks, are not normally protectable. No single company can monopolize their use. Examples include descriptive terms, such as *dependable* or *tasty;* personal or place names, such *as Bob's Barber Shop* or *Downtown Cleaners;* and words that praise the product, such as *Blue Ribbon* or *Tip-Top.* However, names using ordinary words may become protectable if, through long use and extensive public familiarity, they become associated exclusively with one company. *McDonald's* and *Best Foods* are well-known examples.

Companies that create strong trademarks have exclusive use. A strong mark could be a name made up by the company, such as *Exxon* or *Reebok.* Ordinary words used in arbitrary or surprising ways, such as Apple™ computers or Penguin™ books, are also strong marks. Finally, names that are creatively suggestive of the product's qualities, without being merely descriptive, are also strong marks. Examples include the Roach Motel^{SM} pest control and Chicken of the Sea™ tuna.

Once a business chooses a trademark, it should conduct a search to ensure that no other business is already using it. If the mark is already in use, you risk a lawsuit. Businesses can conduct trademark searches themselves, either manually or through computer databases, or they can hire an attorney or trademark search firm.

You can register a mark in any state you use it. In California, for example, you register it with the secretary of state. Registration lasts for ten years. When it expires, you can renew it for an additional ten years.

If you use a mark across state, territorial, or national lines, or will in the near future, register it with the U.S. Patent and Trademark Office. You don't need to register to obtain the protection of trademark laws. Registration, however, gives notice to all would-be copiers that the trademark is in use. Also, those who own registered trademarks can receive higher monetary awards if a dispute over the trademark goes to court.

In most states, if someone uses a trademark without permission, the business that owns the trademark can sue for a court order stopping the use. If the trademark is very distinctive, it isn't necessary to show customer confusion with the similarity. It is sufficient to show that the unauthorized use dilutes the distinctiveness of the mark. You can also stop trademark use without showing customer confusion if the use tends to damage the trademark owner's business reputation.

If you registered the mark and another business uses it to advertise or sell counterfeit goods or services, you can sue for a court order seizing the counterfeit goods.

Copyrights

Federal copyright law gives the creator of an original work of expression, such as a play, song, painting, or book, the right to control how to use that work. A copyright grants a number of specific rights regarding the expression. These include the exclusive right to make copies or authorize others to make copies. They also include the right to make derivative expressions, such as translations or updates, sell the expression, perform or display the expression, and sue others who violate these rights.

A work fixed in tangible form for the first time on or after January 1, 1978, is automatically protected from the moment of its creation. The term is for the author's life, plus an additional fifty years after the author's death. For joint works prepared by two or more authors who did not work for hire, the term is fifty years after the last surviving author's death. Other rules apply to works made for hire, and for anonymous and pseudonymous works, unless the Copyright Office records reveal the author's identity. The copyright duration for these is seventy-five years from publication or one hundred years from creation, whichever is shorter.

There is no *international copyright* that will automatically protect an author's works throughout the entire world. Protection against unauthorized use in a particular country depends on the laws of that country. However, most countries do offer protection to foreign works under certain conditions. International copyright treaties and conventions have greatly simplified these conditions. Request Circular 38a from the U.S. Copyright Office for a list of countries that maintain copyright relations with the United States. Write or call the Copyright Office at

Register of Copyrights
Library of Congress
Washington, DC 20540
(202) 707-9100 Forms Hotline

Under the *fair-use* rule of copyright law, an author may make limited use of another author's work without asking permission. The fair-use privilege is perhaps the most significant limitation on a copyright owner's exclusive rights.

Subject to some general limitations, the following are fair-use examples:

- Criticism and comment—for example, quoting or excerpting a work in a review or criticism for purposes of illustration or comment
- News reporting—for example, summarizing an address or article, with brief quotations, in a news report
- Research and scholarship—for example, quoting a short passage in a scholarly, scientific, or technical work for illustration or clarification of the author's observations
- Nonprofit educational uses—for example, photocopying of limited portions of written works by teachers for classroom use

In most other situations, copying is not legally a fair use. Without an author's permission, such a use violates the author's copyright. Uses motivated by desire for commercial gain cause most violations. Publishing a work primarily for private commercial gain weighs against a finding of fair use.

Copyright law covers literary works, computer software, musical arrangements, graphic works, audiovisual works, and compilations of these. The work must be in some way original. A copyright does not protect merely clerical or factual works, such as a blank form or the phone book. The facts or ideas expressed are not themselves protected by copyright—only the way the creator has expressed those facts or ideas. For example, anyone is free to write a book about a subject that other books have already covered. However, the author of a new book cannot legally copy language from an earlier book.

A copyright notice tells the world that the creator of the work is claiming a copyright. A complete notice consists of the © symbol or the word *copyright* or *copr.*, the year of publication, and the name of the copyright owner. Works published before March 1, 1989, must have a copyright notice to maintain the copyright in the work. Works published after that date don't require a notice. However, even if you don't legally need to give notice, place a copyright notice on your work to warn others that you are protecting your work. It will help you enforce your copyright in court if necessary.

You can register your copyright with the Register of Copyrights located at the Library of Congress, Washington, DC. To get the full benefits of registration, you must register within three months of the date of publication, or before an infringement has begun. Timely registration makes it easier to prove and win an infringement action in federal court and to recover enough money to make the lawsuit worthwhile. You must register before you can bring a lawsuit for infringement of copyright.

Patents

A patent is the legal right, granted by the U.S. Patent and Trademark Office, to exclude others from making, using, or selling an invention. It is valid for up to twenty years from the date you file the application for a patent. A patent deed is the certificate that grants the patent and describes the invention. If someone infringes on your patent by marketing your invention, you may sue in federal court for the economic loss you suffer.

There are three types of patents:

- **Utility patents** cover inventions that work uniquely to produce a *utilitarian result*. Most items that perform a function fall under this category. A utility patent lasts for twenty years from the date of filing.
- **Design patents** cover unique, ornamental, or visible shapes or designs of objects. Inventions that are aesthetic rather than functional—such as a computer screen icon—fall into this category. A design patent lasts for fourteen years.
- **Plant patents** cover new strains of plants. These patents last for seventeen years.

You can't patent everything. For example, you can't patent an abstract idea, a purely mental process, or a process that you can simply perform using a pencil and paper. You can't patent naturally occurring things. To be patentable, an invention must be a process, a machine, a manufacture, a composition, or an improvement on one of these. Each of these categories includes a wide variety of items, from computer software to genetically engineered bacteria.

An invention must satisfy three additional requirements to be patentable:

- **Novelty.** The invention must be a new idea, physically different in at least some small way from what already exists. Inventors' circles call this *prior art*.
- **Non-obviousness.** The invention must be a new or unexpected development. This means something that, at the time of its invention, would not be obvious to a person skilled in the technology of that particular field.
- **Usefulness.** The invention must have some positive use or, in the case of a design patent, must be ornamental. This requirement precludes, for example, inventions that have only illegal uses, or drugs that have only unsafe uses.

To obtain a patent, submit a detailed application to the U.S. Patent and Trademark Office. File your application within one year of the first commercialization of your invention or the first publication of the details of your invention. It generally takes eighteen to twenty-four months to obtain a patent.

Trade Secrets

A trade secret is any information that provides a competitive advantage because competitors don't know the information. It is important that the business take reasonable precautions to keep others from learning the secret. A trade secret can be a formula, process, device, or even a unique compilation of information, such as a marketing list. The owner of trade-secret information can sue to prevent use of the information by anyone who has wrongfully acquired it.

Reasonable precautions include

- Restricting access to the secrets, through the use of passwords, codes, and restricted locations
- Posting warnings and telling all employees that the information is considered a trade secret and must be kept confidential
- Using nondisclosure agreements, which require persons to whom trade secrets must be disclosed for business purposes to obtain proper authorization before disclosing the trade secret
- Using confidentiality agreements, by which employees agree not to disclose trade secrets
- Using tightly drafted and specific noncompetition or nonsolicitation agreements that are legally enforceable

If someone steals or uses a trade secret, the business can sue both the thief and the ultimate user of the information, usually a new employer, for trade-secret infringement. The business can request an injunction preventing use of the trade secret. The business can also ask for monetary compensation for profits improperly made by use of the protected information, or profits lost as a result of the theft.

MISCELLANEOUS LEGAL CONCERNS

There are a variety of miscellaneous legal issues you may deal with on a regular basis, or may only need to deal with infrequently, if at all. Here are some issues to consider:

Contract and sales law

Understand general contract and sales law principles. Take a business law class or read a good business law book so that you understand the basics. Put all your important agreements in writing and cover all the contingencies and conditions. Read all contracts. Use your lawyer prudently for major decisions and for reviewing documents.

Business and professions law

Partnerships and corporations have separate state laws that apply to them. In addition, many occupations and professions also have more specific state laws that apply. Do your research. Check with your attorney, industry trade associations, and the state regulatory agencies.

Securities law

Whenever you separate ownership and management, you likely have a security. Stocks, bonds, and limited partnership interests are almost always securities. General partnership interests and promissory notes can be securities. Be aware that complex federal and state laws govern the issuance of securities. Exemptions are often available from the most onerous rules, but be very careful. Obtain proper legal advice. Be particularly careful when dealing with out-of-state investors, investors you don't have a preexisting relationship with, unsophisticated investors, and anytime you plan to publicly solicit investors. Talk with an experienced securities lawyer before starting.

Credit laws

Become familiar with any state credit laws and with the six major federal credit laws. Here is a brief description of the six federal laws:

- **Equal Credit Opportunity Act** (as amended in 1977). Prohibits discrimination in granting credit on the basis of race, national origin, religion, age, sex, marital status, receipt of public assistance.
- **Fair Credit Reporting Act** (as amended in 1994). Requires credit bureau reports to contain accurate, relevant, and recent information, and regulates access, review, and corrections.

- **Fair Credit Billing Act** (1975). Sets rules for credit card billing policies, error corrections, and inquiries.
- **Consumer Credit Protection Act** (Truth in Lending as amended in 1982). Requires disclosure of dollar amount of finance charges and annual percentage rate, and limits liability for stolen and lost cards to fifty dollars per card.
- **Fair Debt Collection Practices Act** (1978). Regulates and restricts actions of debt collection businesses.
- **Fair Credit and Charge Card Disclosure Act** (1988). Requires full disclosure of all fees, grace periods, and other terms.

Also, familiarize yourself with your state usury laws. These limit the amount of interest you may charge on certain loans.

Consumer protection laws

Become familiar with state and federal laws designed to provide protection to consumers. There are laws regulating advertising, labeling, warranties, door-to-door sales, mail order, deliveries, and repairs. In addition, certain products or industries have laws specifically geared to them. Automobiles, appliances, carpeting, hearing aids, timeshares, health clubs, auctions, and charities are a few common examples. Again, do your research so that you are aware of rules and restrictions.

Antitrust laws

Federal and state antitrust laws govern these areas:

- Illegal price fixing
- Refusals to deal with a competitor, supplier, or customer
- Charging different prices to different customers
- Certain territorial restraints
- Attempts to create monopolies
- Other areas that restrain competition and interfere with the operation of the free market

Often thought to apply only to large businesses, certain anticompetitive practices may even subject a small business to liability. In particular, product manufacturers and distributors need to seek legal counsel experienced in these matters.

Worker safety laws

The federal Occupational Safety and Health Organization (OSHA) and the state equivalents have many laws and regulations designed for employee safety. Make sure you know and comply with the rules. Keep appropriate records.

Pension and fringe benefit laws

Complex tax and labor rules govern the creation and use of pension and fringe benefit plans. Owners often want to set up plans that benefit only them, or benefit them to a much greater extent than the regular employees. Many of the laws prevent or limit such desires. Don't venture into this area without experienced legal and tax assistance.

Franchise and business opportunity laws

There are strict federal and state laws that regulate franchises and business opportunities. There are also prohibitions against *pyramid schemes.* Operators of multilevel or network marketing programs should review these. Check with an expert if you think your business might be subject to such laws.

Americans with Disabilities Act (ADA)

This federal law took effect in 1992 and aims to prevent discrimination in the hiring, promotion, and accommodation of the disabled. The act mandates access for the disabled to "public accommodation," defined to include inns, restaurants, entertainment facilities, retail establishments, grocery stores, service businesses, public transportation, schools, and places of exercise or recreation. In some limited instances, the act grants exemptions if compliance would result in an undue burden, or would not be readily achievable.

Employers of fifteen or more employees must make "reasonable accommodations" to enable disabled individuals to perform the "essential functions" of their jobs without imposing "undue hardship" on the employer. "Reasonable accommodation" may include providing special equipment, restructuring the job to enable the individual to perform its essential functions, or making the job site accessible to the disabled. This act will become even more important in future years.

CHAPTER 16
ACTION ITEMS

Legal Start-up Issues

1. Determine the specific licensing and tax requirements that apply to your business.

2. Describe the specific intellectual property issues that you will need to consider.

3. Describe all other important laws to consider in your business.

CHAPTER 17

Personnel Management

Delegating work and motivating employees to accomplish results can dramatically increase your business productivity and financial success. To really grow a business, you need to leverage people and money. However, dealing with employee problems and concerns can also be one of the entrepreneur's biggest headaches.

You and any co-owners need to clearly focus from the beginning on what your goals and desires are in this start-up enterprise. Are you content with a "lifestyle" business with few employee problems, or do you want the potential growth and increased financial success that comes with proper utilization of employees?

Whether or not you plan to have employees now, sometime, or never, it is a good idea to prepare a formal organization chart by position. Think long range into the future as to how you see your business when your dreams do come true. Even though you may be doing all the work by yourself now, forget that. Diagram an organization chart with a box for every position you reasonably see as a potential "job." This might range from the CEO to the janitor. Make logical connections for lines of authority, responsibility, and communication. Most of these connections will reasonably break down into the three major divisions of operations, marketing, and finance. You can then further divide these.

After you have completed the chart, start at the bottom and write a job description for each position. Assign responsibility for each position to the appropriate person. Obviously you may be in all positions if you're a sole proprietor with no current employees. That's fine for now. This is a work in progress. As you perform all the jobs and learn more about them, augment the job description. Eventually you will fill some positions with other people, starting from the bottom and working up the chart. Having performed the tasks yourself, and having written down a description of duties, you are in an excellent position to recruit, hire, and train the right person for the job.

Keep in mind that your customer should really be at the top of the organization chart. Your business exists to satisfy customers' wants and needs. If you keep your customers happy, you keep your customers, and you stay in business. If you stray from the customer satisfaction concept, the business is in trouble. Make sure all employees understand and agree with this philosophy.

This chapter discusses recruiting and hiring appropriate and talented employees. It covers managing and compensating them properly, along with avoiding major employment legal problems.

RECRUITING AND HIRING EMPLOYEES

Sometime soon you may need to hire someone to perform certain tasks. If you completed and updated the organization chart previously described, you already have a good initial job description. If not, write a job description for the position before you start looking for someone to fill the position.

Carefully think through everything you need in the job. A proper job description clearly explains the job title, who the person reports to and works with, and what the major duties and responsibilities are. It should list all special qualifications, requirements, and conditions of the job. This includes education, experience, knowledge, skills, and legitimate physical and mental requirements.

The job description should specify what percentage of time the employee normally spends on each part of the job. It should set priorities and clarify the most important parts of the job. It should detail working days, hours, overtime, or special project requirements, and clarify responsibility and authority limits. Also include desired or required attitude and personality traits.

Before deciding how to recruit applicants, determine how many applicants you want to interview, how you want them to respond (phone, letter, visit), and your salary range and flexibility. Select the criteria you will use to evaluate their potential.

The best way to fill a position is with someone you already know, or with someone you find through personal contacts or word of mouth. Certainly consider promoting within the company if appropriate. If there are no possibilities through these methods, here are some other methods of recruiting applicants along with some tips:

Classified ads. Use specialized papers and trade journals for special skills. Use the Sunday classifieds for more general requirements. Many nonqualified people may apply, so word the ad clearly and set up a screening system. Give thought to the best category or job title(s) to list the job. Specify the method of response you want from the applicant.

Private employment agencies and search firms. Clarify the agency fee amount and payment responsibility. Decide whether you can justify using an agency or search firm to save you time, money, and energy. Obtain references from satisfied clients. Discover what screening, interviewing, and testing methods the agency uses. Look for specialized agencies.

Government agencies. Consider the state and local employment services that tax dollars support. They often offer counseling, screening, testing, and training. There may be financial and tax incentives for employers. This is an often overlooked source.

Schools. Secondary schools, trade schools, colleges, and universities are sources for certain classes of employees, particularly those who need no specific work experience. Some schools and colleges have internship programs that enable students to gain practical experience. They allow the employer to receive services at a lower than usual cost. Schools can be an excellent source of enthusiastic, intelligent part-time employees. Discover whether local schools and colleges have employment or job placement departments. Consider posting a job notice or asking appropriate teachers for recommendations.

Help-wanted signs. This is an inexpensive way to provide wide exposure to those who live near your business. However, it doesn't screen applicants, and it may bring in more applicants than you can efficiently handle. If you utilize it, consider being more specific on the sign as to what type of help and what qualifications you need. Consider posting signs in appropriate neighboring locations, as well as in your location.

Walk-ins and mail-ins. If you already are a well-established business, you frequently have people walk in and ask if you are hiring or send you unsolicited letters and resumes. If you have time, obtain some basic information from the walk-ins, and ask them a few questions. Keep a file of interested candidates. An opportunity may arise later even if nothing is currently available. Treat everyone courteously whether or not you have openings.

Current employee referrals. Your current employees may provide excellent job prospect referrals. You hope they will not recommend applicants they believe to be incompatible with the business and company culture, or inferior in ability, because it will reflect on them. Asking employees shows that you respect their opinion. However, beware of good-friend recommendations that may have more of a social interest. Think about how you will explain any rejections of referrals. Consider using financial awards or other incentives for successful referrals.

Friends and relatives. Your own friends and relatives, as well as friends and relatives of colleagues, associates, and other contacts, can be a great source of prospective employees. However, there can be many problems as well. Some may not be qualified. There may be jealousy or resentment among other employees. There may be family and friend conflict created outside the job. This issue will come up regularly during your business existence. Consider how you will handle the issue before it arises. Follow a consistent policy.

Temporary help agencies. Using a temporary agency can be an ideal solution if you need someone only at certain times during the year or for an immediate, temporary project. You can call the agency, explain your needs, and often have someone available immediately. If the person does not work out, ask for someone else. You pay for this simplicity, but it saves you the time, cost, energy, and paperwork of hiring and dealing with payroll. It is also a way to view performance before making a longer-term hiring decision. Clarify the agency rules on offering someone regular employment.

Competitors. For specialized skills, employees working for related or competitive businesses may be your best candidates. They already have training, and they understand the industry. However, hiring may create bad feelings between you and the competitor. The competitor may also hire your employees. Make sure you do not violate any laws, interfere with any contracts, or encourage any prospective employee to violate an employment contract. Be aware of potential claims for violation of confidential information, trade secrets, and covenants not to compete. Consult your lawyer if you have any questions.

Internet and computer databases. These may signal the future of job hunting and job matching. Keep up with the latest techniques and technology related to your business.

Employee leasing. *Leasing* employees from a legitimate employee leasing firm rather than hiring employees is similar to leasing equipment rather than owning it. It is a valid way to minimize bookkeeping, payroll, and fringe benefits by paying the leasing firm a premium to cover such costs. However, you may have to do the recruiting, screening, and "hiring" yourself.

Develop a complete employment application form that collects the basic data you need. Obtain specific information on employment and education background, and the specific skills and abilities needed for the job. Don't ask for legally inappropriate information. Have your attorney review the application.

During the interview with an applicant, follow a logical and planned sequence. Know exactly what you want to accomplish during the interview. Conduct the interview in a quiet atmosphere. Establish rapport, make the applicant feel at ease, and give your entire attention to the applicant. Listen attentively. Don't argue or show disapproval. The candidate should be talking much more than you. Closely observe the applicant's speech, mannerisms, and attire if these are important to the job. Look for a *results orientation* in the candidate's responses to questions about prior work and successes. Look for the desire to work hard and to start immediately. Is the candidate prepared? Does the candidate ask intelligent questions? What does your intuition tell you?

Brian Tracy, renowned business management speaker and trainer, strongly suggests that you interview at least three candidates for any job. If feasible, interview a candidate at least three times.

Interview them in at least three different situations. Use at least three different or additional interviewers if your firm size allows it. This prevents any hasty decisions. Also, check at least three referrals. Phone personally and try to talk to the person who worked most directly with the candidate. Ask about the candidate's strengths and weaknesses. Ask for any other information that the respondent feels you should know about the candidate.

Keep detailed notes of all interviews and all discussions with references. This assists you in remembering each candidate accurately so that you can make a reasoned decision. It could also prove useful if any discrimination or other legal claims arise later.

Before making a job offer to a candidate, make sure you like the person and that the candidate will fit in well with your business and culture. Ensure that the candidate desires to work there, can contribute, and wants to contribute. Encourage the candidate to carefully think it over before making a final decision. Neither party should act in haste. It's much better to make a well-reasoned decision at this stage than to discover problems later. Make sure the compensation and benefits are clear and acceptable.

Heed the "Seven Steps of Learning to Read People," that author and executive Mark H. McCormack lists in his informative and entertaining book, *What They Don't Teach You at Harvard Business School*. These tips are valuable in all interpersonal contacts:

1. Listen aggressively. Pay attention to both *what* they say and *how* they say it.
2. Observe aggressively. Pay attention to motions, gestures, and dress.
3. Talk less. Ask questions and then listen.
4. Take a second look at first impressions. They may be incorrect.
5. Take time to use what you've learned. Think before acting.
6. Be discreet. Don't let them know what you know.
7. Be detached. *Act* rather than *react*. Be the controller rather than the one being controlled. If you don't react, you will never overreact.

Managing and Compensating Employees

There are probably as many management theories in the business world as there are management books. New theories appear regularly. Old theories go in and out of vogue. Management, in its simplest form, consists of delegating work to be done by others and motivating them to do it. This section discusses one simple and effective theory: the "One Minute Manager" theory first espoused by Kenneth Blanchard and Spencer Johnson in their landmark book, *The One Minute Manager*.

Forming clear and detailed job descriptions, and filling the positions with good employees with potential, are the important first requirements. You need to give new employees clear direction by telling them what you want, when you want it, and how to do it. As they progress and learn the job, change from *directing* to *delegating*. Assign the results you expect, give authority to accomplish such results, and design a follow-up system that allows you to inspect what you expect.

The three secrets of the one minute manager are one minute goal setting, one minute praisings, and one minute reprimands. Knowing the basic concepts and steps and tailoring them to your specific situation is a good start in simple yet effective management techniques.

One Minute Goal Setting consists of getting together with your employee to

- Agree on no more than three major goals.
- Have the employee concisely write out each goal on paper.
- Encourage the employee to read and reread each goal regularly.
- Regularly compare performance to goals.

One Minute Praisings consist of the following steps:

- Praise immediately when justified.
- Be specific about what the employee did right.
- Tell employees how good you feel about what they did right and how it helps the organization and the other employees.
- Stop for a moment of silence to let them *feel* how good you feel.
- Encourage them to do more of the same.

One Minute Reprimands consist of the following steps:

- Reprimand immediately when justified.
- Be specific about what they did wrong.

- Tell the employee clearly how you feel about what they did wrong and how it affects the organization and others.
- Stop for a moment of uncomfortable silence to let them *feel* how you feel.
- Remind them of how much you value and think of them as people. It's only their performance that you are criticizing.

Feedback is the "breakfast of champions." Employees need positive feedback, especially in the early days of a new job. Provide it when they are learning, even if they are performing tasks only *approximately* right. Don't use reprimands for people just learning or in training. Save reprimands for those who know what and how they should do things, but are just not performing up to expectations. Praise in public. Reprimand in private.

Develop a consistent, legally sound progressive discipline system. Adequately document everything to protect yourself. Be honest and fair in performance appraisals and discipline. Treat everyone the same so that there are no claims of special treatment. Put your time and energy into hiring well in the first place, so you will rarely need to use discipline or termination.

Knowledge is power in negotiating compensation and other benefits. Know exactly what the job is worth, what others are paying for similar duties, and how much you can afford to pay. Everyone has a comfort level range of pay that satisfies them. Try to pay at the lower end of the comfort level. If someone is currently unemployed, they are less likely to challenge your compensation offer. If they are leaving an existing job, expect to pay at least 10 percent more than they currently make. Try to obtain prior salary history on their job application. Don't be cheap, but don't pay more than you have to pay, especially for lower-level positions.

Use some personal selling and promotion skills in describing and explaining the compensation. Clearly show the monetary value of payroll taxes and fringe benefits that truly benefit the employee. Consider probationary periods and regular reviews with possible salary increases.

Put monetary compensation in the proper perspective. Studies show that most employers believe the most important factors to an employee are salary, benefits, job security, and working conditions. These are clearly very important. However, after such needs have been substantially met, many employees really look for and need low-cost or no-cost intangible benefits. These include praise, recognition, opportunity for advancement, and a feeling of accomplishment and satisfaction.

A Gallup Organization survey showed that the most critical factors bearing on employees' satisfaction and job performance are the following:

- At work, employees have the opportunity every day to do what they do best.
- A supervisor or someone at work seems to care about them as people.
- At work, employees' opinions seem to count.
- Over the past year, employees had opportunities to learn and grow.
- The mission of the employer makes employees feel that their jobs are important.
- Employees have the materials and equipment to do their work right.
- Employees' companies are "family friendly."

Besides salary and wages for services performed, here are some other tangible and intangible *benefits* to consider as additional compensation:

- Bonuses and incentive compensation
- Overtime pay and compensatory time off
- Vacations and holidays
- Direct deposit and savings programs
- Company stock as current compensation
- Stock options, stock appreciation rights, or other deferred contingent ownership plans
- Tangible and intangible performance, safety, and attendance awards
- Company parties, picnics, athletic teams, and casual dress days
- Company store and company product discounts
- Fringe benefits such as health care, child care, life insurance, tuition reimbursement, free parking, recreational facilities, and on-site cafeteria
- Free food, juice, coffee, and soft drinks
- Flexible work schedule

- Deferred compensation plans, pension and profit-sharing plans, and employee stock ownership plans
- Company matching employee pension contributions
- Career education and training
- Good physical and social work environment
- Career opportunities and a long-term chance for growth and development
- Opportunity to learn and to develop new skills
- Promotional opportunities upward and laterally
- Responsibility
- Autonomy
- Personal sense of well-being from accomplishments
- Managerial praise
- Job security
- Positive feedback from customers
- Respect from coworkers

Learn as much as you can about your employees. Harvey Mackay's list of the thirty-three things you should know is a good starting point. Review the "Mackay 33™ for Managers" in *Beware the Naked Man Who Offers You His Shirt*. There is also an excellent checklist for employees to use when evaluating employers ("Mackay 33™ for Employees").

EMPLOYMENT LEGAL CONCERNS

Hiring your first employee immediately subjects your business to many federal and state laws. As you hire more employees, additional laws may apply. The rules and related paperwork complicate life. This is one major reason "lifestyle" entrepreneurs often choose not to hire employees.

This section highlights and briefly explains the major employment legal considerations. Consult with your attorney on specifics. Both federal and state laws apply, the laws are constantly changing, and the laws may or may not apply depending on size, industry, and other factors. This section also covers in detail the very important, yet confusing, issue of independent contractor versus employee.

Be aware of the general concerns expressed in the following laws:

Child labor. Laws restrict the type, days, and hours of work for children under age eighteen.

Discrimination. Federal law applies to businesses with fifteen or more employees. It prohibits hiring, firing, or promotion decisions based on race, skin color, gender, religious beliefs, national origin, age forty or over, pregnancy, and disability. State laws are often even more strict. California law, for example, applies to businesses with five or more employees. It additionally prohibits discrimination based on marital status, sexual preference, HIV or AIDS, political activities, and arrests. Make sure you base all employment decisions on relevant education, experience, and skills. Relate all tests to specific job duties and required skills.

Drug testing. Check current federal and state laws and cases for rules and limitations on requiring new or existing employees to submit to regular or special drug testing.

English-only rules. Check current federal and state laws and cases for rules and limitations that require employees to speak only English on the job.

Equal pay. You must pay all employees equally in compensation and fringe benefits for substantially equal work, regardless of gender. Justify any compensation differences by a factor other than gender, such as seniority, merit, quantity of production, or quality of production.

Family and medical leave. Federal and state laws generally apply to employers with fifty or more employees and require granting a certain amount of unpaid leave for family and medical problems.

Firing. The rule of "employment at will" allows employers to terminate employees for any reason as long as it is not an improper reason. Improper reasons include breach of an express or implied contract, violation of a specific law, and violation of public policy. There are numerous federal and state laws that, if violated by the employer, constitute wrongful termination. Common examples include discharge based on any of the following:

- Illegal discrimination
- Union membership
- Filing a workers' compensation claim
- Reporting employer violations of laws
- Refusal to work in an unsafe workplace

- Serving on a jury
- Having wages garnished once
- Having filed bankruptcy

Health and safety regulations. Federal and state laws protect workers' rights to safe and healthful work conditions. You must display several specific posters. California and other states require specific Injury and Illness Prevention Programs.

Health insurance. Check current federal and state laws regulating health insurance coverage and continuation. Currently, there is no requirement to offer coverage. However, if you do offer coverage, you generally can't discriminate among employees. There are some exceptions for part-time workers and union workers.

Immigrant workers. All employees must complete INS Form I-9 to prove they can legally work in the United States. They must produce specific documents as proof. Photocopy the documents and maintain good records for all employees.

Lie detector tests. Federal law generally prohibits the use of polygraphs in connection with employment.

Pensions. Check current federal and state laws regulating pension coverage and continuation. Currently, there is no requirement to offer coverage. However, if you do offer a pension plan, complex rules apply. These rules cover discrimination, participation, and vesting.

Personnel files. State laws generally require employers to maintain certain personnel records. They give employees broad access to their files.

Pregnancy. Federal law generally prohibits discrimination against women on the basis of pregnancy, childbirth, or any other medical condition. State laws often have additional protections and restrictions.

Psychological testing. Check current federal and state laws for any restrictions on this type of employment testing. Make sure any tests do not indirectly discriminate on an illegal basis.

Sexual harassment. Sexual harassment on the job is any unwelcome sexual advance or conduct that creates an intimidating, hostile, or offensive work environment. Both federal and state laws prohibit such behavior. Employers and supervisors are liable for acts of employees on the job. Make sure your business has a strict written policy. Stress its importance and enforce it consistently.

Sick leave. There is no requirement that it be given. If it is, you generally can't discriminate in benefits.

Smoking policies. Check current federal, state, and local laws.

Unemployment insurance. Employer contributions fund this federal and state program based on the first $7,000 of each employee's compensation. Employees who have left their job for "good cause" are generally eligible for unemployment benefits.

Unions. Several major federal labor laws regulate union membership and activities. Don't interfere, restrain, or coerce employees in any union decisions or activities.

Vacations. There is no requirement that it be given. If it is, you generally can't discriminate in benefits.

Wage and hour restrictions. There are federal and state minimum wage and overtime laws, compensatory time and final paycheck laws.

Workers' compensation. This no-fault employer-funded insurance program covers workers injured on the job. Benefits to injured workers include medical treatment, temporary disability pay, permanent disability compensation, and vocational rehabilitation.

The issue of independent contractors versus employees is one of the most misunderstood and dangerous areas in business. Improper classification can cause problems that financially destroy your business. Thus, it's important to know the rules and related risks.

The key factor that determines whether a worker is an independent contractor is, who has the right to control the worker as to how the worker accomplishes the task(s)? The *right* to control is important—not whether you actually exert control. If a hiring firm controls the *means* by which the worker does the task(s), the worker is automatically an employee. If the hiring firm can exercise control only as to the *results* of the work, the worker is usually an independent contractor.

It's sometimes difficult to define what control means. Therefore, you need to analyze twenty common-law factors to make a proper decision. This section discusses those twenty factors later. First, however, it's necessary to explain the importance of distinguishing between the two, and the potential disasters that await your business if you improperly classify the worker.

Businesses try to avoid classifying workers as employees for a variety of reasons. They realize that employees require extra bookkeeping and paperwork, payroll tax obligations, and tax withholding obligations. Thus, it is simpler to classify someone an independent contractor, and make direct payments to them. However, it doesn't matter what you *call* someone, it's what they *are* under all the facts and circumstances that counts.

Potential problems that can result from improper classification include the following:

- The IRS, the state employment tax agency, and other taxing authorities can make claims for unpaid payroll taxes, penalties, and interest. In addition, the IRS and the state income tax agency can make claims against the employer for income taxes that the employer did not properly withhold from the worker's payments. This applies even though such taxes are the obligation of the worker.

- Employees are subject to various protective laws, such as minimum wage, overtime, and child labor limits, that independent contractors are not.

- Unemployment taxes paid by the employer cover employees. Such taxes don't cover independent contractors. However, a so-called independent contractor may later make claims for unemployment benefits. This could be disastrous for the business. If an agency or court determines the business should have covered the worker, that business is liable for payment of the unemployment benefits. Such a claim often subjects the business to a complete audit as to all workers.

- Workers' compensation covers employees injured on the job. The business pays the premium. Independent contractors are responsible for their own insurance. The hiring firm does not cover them. However, if the so-called independent contractor incurs an injury on the job and makes a claim for benefits, there is a problem. Litigation may occur. It is expensive and time consuming, no matter what the result. An agency or court may hold the business liable for such workers' compensation benefits.

- The legal doctrine of "respondeat superior" holds that an employer is liable for the acts of employees incurred within the scope of employment. However, hiring firms are not liable for the acts of independent contractors. Problems can result if the so-called independent contractor injures an innocent third party. Often, the lawsuit will name both the independent contractor and the hiring firm, claiming that the so-called independent contractor was actually an employee. The hiring firm could be liable if an agency or court determines that the worker is an employee. Additionally, the business's insurance company would likely deny coverage since the business never informed them that the worker was an employee.

- Employees can bring wrongful termination actions if they believe their employer terminated them for a discriminatory or an illegal reason. Independent contractors are subject to basic contract principles, not to the complex and ever-changing principles of wrongful termination actions.

- Employers must often cover employees for fringe benefits, pension plans, vacation pay, and other benefits. Employers do not cover independent contractors for such benefits.

Any of the above claims could financially destroy a business. Even if the business eventually prevails, the time, expense, and stress in defending actions are very burdensome.

Now that you understand the serious problems that can befall you by erroneously classifying an employee as an independent contractor, how do you correctly determine status?

It's not easy. Each government entity has its own special rules for making such a classification. A worker could be an employee under one set of rules and an independent contractor under others.

Additionally, some workers are *statutory employees*. These workers are automatically employees for certain payroll tax purposes because of special laws. There are other workers who are *statutory independent contractors* under the tax law. Consult both federal and state income and payroll tax laws, depending upon your specific situation.

For the workers who don't fall under the statutory employee or statutory independent contractor rules, the IRS has developed a test using twenty factors. The IRS uses this test on a case-by-case basis to determine whether a worker is an independent contractor or an employee. Other government entity and common-law tests are similar, but not identical.

The IRS uses these twenty factors to measure how much control the hiring firm has over its worker. Typically, companies have the right to exert substantial control over employees, but little control over independent contractors. For example, a hiring firm can't direct their outside office supply representative in the same way that they can direct an employee from their own supply department. Remember that the government is looking to see if the hiring firm has the *right* to exert control—it does not care whether the firm actually exerted that control.

Independent contractors do not have to satisfy all twenty common-law factors. Think of the factors as weights on a balance scale. For a hiring firm to prove that a worker is an independent contractor, most of the factors weighed must be on the independent contractor's side of the scale. If some factors lean toward the employee side, the hiring firm must show that other factors, or a factor with more weight, offset them.

For specific industries and specific cases, check the IRS revenue rulings, IRS private-letter rulings, and relevant case law. Courts have given different weights for each factor according to the industry and job. The courts have not always been consistent in weighing the twenty factors. There are contradictory cases you can't reconcile. The decision is often subjective.

Here are the twenty common-law factors. A prototype of the "perfect" independent contractor would reflect the following:

Factor 1. No instructions

Contractors don't need to follow instructions to accomplish a job. Employers don't furnish them with instructions. However, the hiring firm may provide job specifications to them.

Factor 2. No training

Contractors do not receive training by the hiring firm. They use their own methods to accomplish the work.

Factor 3. Services don't have to be rendered personally

Businesses hire contractors to provide a result. Contractors have the right to hire others to do the actual work.

Factor 4. Work not essential to the hiring firm

A company's success or continuation should not depend on the service of outside contractors. An example violating this factor would be a law firm that called their lawyers independent contractors.

Factor 5. Own work hours

Contractors set their own work hours.

Factor 6. Not a continuing relationship

Contractors usually don't have a continuing relationship with a hiring company. The relationship can be frequent, but it must be at irregular intervals, on call, or whenever work is available. Part-time, seasonal, or short-duration relationships have nothing to do with independent contractor status.

Factor 7. Control their own assistants

Contractors shouldn't hire, supervise, or pay assistants at the direction of the hiring company. If a contractor hires assistants, it should be at the contractor's sole discretion.

Factor 8. Time to pursue other work

Contractors should have enough time available to pursue other gainful work.

Factor 9. Job location

Contractors control where they work. If they work on the premises of the hiring company, it is not under that company's direction or supervision.

Factor 10. Order of work set

Contractors determine the order and sequence in which they will perform their work.

Factor 11. No interim reports

Businesses hire contractors for the final result only. They should not ask contractors for progress or interim reports.

Factor 12. Payment timing

Businesses pay contractors by the job, not by time. Payment by the job can include periodic payments based on a percentage of job completed. However, a business can base payment on the number of hours needed to do the job times a fixed hourly rate. It is best to determine the payment method before the job commences.

Factor 13. Working for multiple firms

Contractors often work for more than one firm at a time.

Factor 14. Business expenses

Contractors are responsible for their own business expenses.

Factor 15. Own tools

Contractors usually furnish their own tools. Some hiring firms have leased equipment to their independent contractors so that they could show that the contractor had his or her own tools and an investment in the business. This strategy won't work if the lease is for a nominal amount or if the hiring firm can void the lease at will. The lease must be equivalent to what an independent business person could have obtained in the open market.

Factor 16. Significant investment

Contractors should be able to perform their services without the hiring company's facilities (equipment, office furniture, machinery, and so forth). The contractor's investment in the trade must be real, essential, and adequate.

Factor 17. Services available to general public

Contractors make their services available to the general public by one or more of the following:

- Having an office and assistants
- Having business signs
- Having a business license
- Listing their services in a business directory
- Advertising their services

Factor 18. Possible profit or loss

Contractors should be able to make a profit or loss. Employees can't suffer a loss. Five circumstances show that a profit or loss is possible:

- The contractor hires, directs, and pays assistants.
- The contractor has an office, equipment, materials, or facilities.
- The contractor has continuing and reoccurring liabilities.
- The contractor has agreed to perform specific jobs for prices agreed upon in advance.
- The contractor's services affect his or her own business reputation.

Factor 19. Limited right to discharge

Businesses can't fire contractors as long as they produce a result that meets the contract specifications.

Factor 20. No compensation for noncompletion

Contractors are responsible for the satisfactory completion of a job. If they fail to complete it, they have legal liability to the hiring firm.

A federal "safe harbor" rule can exempt certain workers from the twenty common-law factors. To be exempt, the following three statements must be true:

- The business consistently treated the worker and similar workers as independent contractors.
- The business filed all the required forms.
- The business had some reasonable basis for treating the worker as an independent contractor. This could be because
    - There were similar rulings or court cases.

     – It was an industrywide practice.

     – Prior tax auditors never questioned the practices.

There are cases where workers are clearly independent contractors. However, when it is probable that they are employees, and when it is uncertain or questionable, classify them as employees. Complete the extra paperwork. Pay the payroll taxes, insurance premiums, and benefits. You will sleep more soundly at night. Such expenses are costs of doing business. Factor them into your business and pricing decisions just as other business expenses.

If a worker clearly is an independent contractor, draft and execute a complete independent contractor agreement. Have the worker complete and sign IRS Form W-9, Request for Taxpayer ID Number and Certification. Realize, however, that interested and affected parties can challenge any agreement, no matter how well you drafted it, or how clearly you explained it. An agency or court could still classify a worker as an employee if the specific facts and circumstances justify that conclusion, even if both parties clearly agree otherwise.

Err on the conservative side. This issue will not go away. It continues to be a big tax and money generator for government entities and third parties pursuing the uninformed business owner.

CHAPTER 17
ACTION ITEMS

Personnel Management

1. Describe and explain the most appropriate ways for your business to recruit new employees.

2. Develop a comprehensive, fair, and creative compensation package for your future employees.

3. Draft a brief independent contractor agreement that protects you and your business.

CHAPTER 18

Accounting and Financial Management

Profitable and liquid—your business must be both to become and remain a success. Keeping accurate records for your business is the first step. Properly analyzing and acting on the data is the next. This chapter discusses the qualities of a good bookkeeping system that allows you to prepare accurate and timely financial statements. It also reviews several financial analysis methods and suggests techniques for efficiently managing cash and minimizing income taxes.

BOOKKEEPING AND FINANCIAL STATEMENTS

There are several reasons why you need to set up and utilize a good bookkeeping system to produce accurate financial statements. Foremost is the benefit to you of having data to analyze, compare, and use to make your business more profitable and more successful. Acting without accurate data or just guessing is dangerous to the health of your business.

You need accurate and reliable bookkeeping to report results and activities to government agencies. Possible agencies include

- Internal Revenue Service (IRS)
- State income taxing authorities
- Employment, property, and sales tax reporting authorities
- Workers' Compensation Board
- Securities and Exchange Commission (SEC)
- State securities agencies
- Federal Trade Commission (FTC)
- Department of Labor (DOL)

It's also a prerequisite to obtaining bank or investor financing. In the early years of the business, it can assist in proving to the IRS that you are operating a *business*, and not a *hobby*.

A good bookkeeping system encompasses a consistent method of documenting, recording, and organizing transactions. It ends with the ability to develop useful financial activity reports from the documented, recorded, and organized transactions.

The first step, documenting, requires you to have some proof of a transaction. Always use a pure business checking account. Don't commingle personal funds. For sales, develop a consecutively numbered invoice or sales receipt system. Deposit all checks and cash in your business account on a regular basis. Ensure that you can justify and accurately describe and document all amounts you deposit. Don't develop the bad habit of taking cash out for personal use and only depositing the net amount.

For payments, use checks as often as possible. If you must pay cash, obtain a receipt, and reimburse yourself from the business checking account later. For small amounts, use a petty cash system you set up and regularly replenish. Use receipts or notes to keep track of all payments.

Credit cards are an excellent method of paying bills and charges. Don't go over your credit limit, and don't carry a balance if you can help it. The interest rates are very high. For accurate and efficient recordkeeping, however, use four different credit cards. Use one for all business meals and entertainment since you must keep separate records for tax purposes. Use another for all automobile expenses that you will later prorate between business and personal use. Use a third for all other business expenses. Use the fourth card for all nonbusiness personal expenses. Once a month, pay the business card balances from your business checking account.

There are two major benefits of using a credit card for business expenses. It is often more convenient than carrying a checkbook and writing checks, and it allows you to write just one check per month for each card. Additionally, all required data is on the card receipt, in case you later need it for backup documentation in a tax audit. For example, each credit card receipt used for a business meal indicates the facility's name, the date of the activity, and the total amount charged. Develop the habit of writing the name and business relationship of the client or other business acquaintance on the back of the receipt. You then have a perfect record that will withstand audit scrutiny.

Record financial transactions accurately and regularly in chronological order. At a minimum, journals for all payments and receipts need to be maintained. This can be as simple as your checkbook register, which is a form of journal. If you have a substantial number of transactions that are of a certain type, use a special journal for recording them. Unless you are strictly a pay-as-you-go type of business, you will likely want special journals for accounts receivable and accounts payable.

Take a basic bookkeeping course if you don't have some background or experience in this area. Every business owner needs to have some basic knowledge in this area, even if the owner plans to delegate much of the recording and organizing. You need to understand the system to make sense of the data and to avoid being cheated or duped.

The best and most accurate bookkeeping system is the double-entry system. Double-entry allows for accrual basis accounting, which is the generally accepted accounting method that all public companies must use for reporting. Tax reporting also requires accrual basis accounting if you have inventory or fall into several other categories. Double-entry, as its name implies, requires that at least two accounts be affected by every transaction. There are equal debits and credits for each transaction. This makes errors less common, or at least allows you to detect and correct them sooner. You can prepare a balance sheet and an income statement, as well as a cash flow statement, from the records when using double-entry accrual basis accounting. You can also maintain current receivable and payable balances. You make accounting adjustments at the end of the period.

Single-entry accounting with the cash basis method is what you have used with your personal checking account. It merely keeps track of what went in and what went out of the account. There are more chances for mistakes, and it is difficult to prepare accurate balance sheets and income statements without analyzing all recorded transactions. However, for small businesses, it may be a sufficient method, if the double-entry accrual method is too daunting or difficult. Clearly show exactly what cash you started with, what went in, and what went out of the account. Balance to what is in the cash account at the end of the period. If you can do this, a good accountant can decipher the needed data to prepare accurate tax returns and financial statements.

Whatever accounting method you use, set up a chart of accounts with account numbers that apply to your business. Classify the accounts under assets, liabilities, owners' equity, revenues, and expenses. Set up a logical numbering system and include all relevant categories. Leave room for adding some later. Starting all assets with 1, all liabilities with 2, all equity with 3, all revenues with 4, and all expenses with 5 is a logical and often-used method. Consider organizing alphabetically within each classification. Treat each of the categories as a separate account ledger. Organize transactions by category in the ledger, rather than chronologically, as in the journal.

Bookkeeping systems can be as simple or as complex as needed. The important point is to set up a system you understand and can use efficiently. Many small businesses start with a checkbook and the checkbook register alone. There are excellent *one-write* systems available from companies like McBee and Safeguard. They provide checks, journals, and ledgers at very low cost. They also assist in setting up a well-organized system that minimizes the number of times you have to record the same information. There are also many inexpensive computer software programs that you can use alone or in combination with a one-write system. Start simple and work up to more automated systems as you grow and have more transactions. You can also contract with a bookkeeping or accounting firm to perform the necessary functions. IRS Publication 583, Starting a Business and Keeping Records, contains some good tips on keeping records for tax reporting purposes.

After documenting, recording, and organizing all your financial transactions, you may need to make some adjustments for nontransactional items that affect the business. Examples include depreciation, bad debts, ending inventory count, and accrual or deferral of expenses and revenue. These are sophisticated decisions that often require an accountant's assistance.

After you make the necessary adjustments and test the records for accuracy, it is time to prepare the financial statements. You should prepare an income statement, a cash flow statement, and a balance sheet. Ideally, prepare the **income statement** using the accrual method. It will show the following general breakdown for a specific period of time (month, quarter, year):

Gross Sales – Sales Returns and Allowances = Net Sales

Net Sales – Cost of Goods Sold = Gross Profit

Gross Profit – Selling and General and Administrative Expenses = Net Profit

The **cash flow statement** will show the following general breakdown for a specific period of time (month, quarter, year):

Beginning Cash + Cash Receipts = Total Cash Available

Total Cash Available – Cash Paid Out = Ending Cash

The **balance sheet** is a "snapshot" of the business at one point in time. Use double-entry bookkeeping to produce an accurate balance sheet. Break the balance sheet equation into subcategories within the basic equation of Assets = Liabilities + Owners' Equity. A balance sheet is useful to have for analysis, but the two most important statements for small business are the income statement, which indicates profitability, and the cash flow statement, which indicates liquidity. A business must be both profitable and liquid to survive over the long term.

This is a brief overview of a very complex subject. Seriously consider using a professional accountant's services for regular financial statement preparation, financial analysis, tax planning, and tax preparation.

FINANCIAL ANALYSIS

Once you have prepared financial statements, or other financial data, what do you do with them? This section explains three useful formulas for business decisions and lists the most common financial ratios used for analyzing and comparing solvency, efficiency, and profitability.

Break-even analysis is a mathematical technique for analyzing the relationship between sales and fixed and variable costs. Break-even analysis is also a profit-planning tool for calculating the point at which sales will equal total costs. The break-even point is the intersection of the total sales and the total cost lines. This point determines the number of units produced to achieve breakeven. The analysis generally assumes linearity (100 percent variable or 100 percent fixed) of costs. If a firm's costs were all variable, the firm could be profitable from the start. If the firm is to avoid losses, its sales must cover all costs that vary directly with production and all costs that do not change with production levels.

Fixed costs are those expenses associated with the project that you would have to pay whether you sold one unit or 10,000 units. Examples include general office expenses, rent, depreciation, interest, salaries, research and development, and utilities. Variable costs vary directly with the number of units that you sell. Examples include materials, direct labor, postage, packaging, and advertising. Some costs are difficult to classify. As a general guideline, if there is a direct relationship between cost and number of units sold, consider the cost variable. If there is no relationship, then consider the cost fixed.

You construct a break-even chart with a horizontal axis representing units produced and a vertical axis representing sales and costs. Represent fixed costs by a horizontal line since they do not change with the number of units produced. Represent variable costs and sales by upward sloping lines since they vary with the number of units produced and sold. The break-even point is the intersection of the total sales and the total cost lines. Above that point, the firm begins to make a profit, but below that point, it suffers a loss. A sample break-even chart is shown on the next page.

The algebraic equation for break-even analysis consists of four factors. If you know any three of the four, you can solve for the fourth factor. You calculate the break-even amount with the following equation:

Sales Price per Unit x Quantity Sold = Fixed Costs + [Variable Costs per Unit x Quantity Sold]

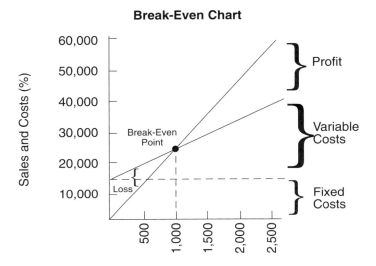

Break-Even Chart

For example, assume you have total fixed monthly costs of $1,200 and total variable costs of $6 per unit. If you could sell the units for $10 each, the equation indicates that you need to sell 300 units to break even. If you knew you could sell 400 units, the equation would indicate that the sales price would need to be $9 per unit to break even.

When managing inventory, you should aim for the *economic order quantity* (EOQ). This is the level of inventory that balances two kinds of inventory costs: holding (or carrying) costs, which increase with the amount of inventory ordered, and order costs, which decrease with the amount ordered.

The largest components of holding costs for most companies are the cost of space to store the inventory and the cost of tying up capital in inventory. Other components include the labor costs associated with inventory maintenance and insurance costs. Also include deterioration, spoilage, and obsolescence costs. The costs of more frequent orders include lost discounts for larger quantity purchases and labor and supply costs of writing the orders. Additional costs include paying the bills and processing the paperwork, associated telephone and mail costs, and the labor costs of processing and inspecting incoming inventory.

EOQ is the size of order that minimizes the total of holding and ordering costs. The algebraic expression of EOQ is as follows:

EOQ = square root of [2 x U x O divided by H] where U is the number of units used annually, O is the order cost per order, and H is the holding cost per unit

For example, assume you use 40,000 units annually, it costs $50 to place an order, and it costs $20 to hold the raw materials for one unit. The equation yields an amount of 447, which is the number of units you need to order at one time to minimize total costs.

The reorder point, or *economic order point* (EOP), tells you when to place an order. Calculating the reorder point requires you to know the lead time from placing to receiving an order. You compute it as follows:

EOP = Lead time x Average usage per unit of time

For example, assume you need 6,400 units evenly throughout the year, there is a lead time of one week, and there are 50 working weeks in the year. You calculate the reorder point to be 128 units as follows.

1 week x [6,400 units / 50 weeks] = 128 units

You might also consider "**just in time**" inventory management, if available and appropriate. "Just in time" allows you to keep minimal inventory in stock. You order only when you make a sale. Carefully analyze the time lag. You must be able to satisfy the customer as well as keep your inventory investment minimized.

Ratio analysis is useful in showing relationships between items on the financial statements. You can use ratio analysis in many ways. You can compare your projections with actual results. You can also compare last year with this year, and last quarter or last month with this quarter or this month. Additional comparisons include same quarters or months of last year with same quarters or months of this year and your business with other similar businesses, or with industry averages.

There are several excellent sources for obtaining pertinent data on similar businesses to use for comparison. Here are several of the most useful sources:

- Dun & Bradstreet's *Industry Norms and Key Business Ratios*, 99 Church Street, New York, NY 10007

- Robert Morris Associates' *Annual Statement Studies*, Philadelphia National Bank Building, Philadelphia, PA 19107
- Accounting Corporation of America's *Barometer of Small Business*, 1929 First Avenue, San Diego, CA 92101
- National Cash Register Company's *Expenses in Retail Businesses*, Marketing Services Department, Dayton, OH 45409
- Small Business Administration (SBA)
- Trade associations

Ratio analysis can assist you in determining solvency, efficiency, or profitability. Here are nine of the most common and important ratios to use in your comparisons:

Solvency Ratios

Quick ratio. Cash plus marketable securities plus accounts receivable divided by total current liabilities.

Current liabilities are all the liabilities that fall due within one year. This ratio, also called the acid-test ratio, reveals the protection afforded short-term creditors in cash or near-cash assets. It shows the number of dollars of liquid assets available to cover each dollar of current debt. Any time this ratio is 1:1 or higher, the business is in a liquid condition. Larger ratios indicate greater liquidity.

Current ratio. Total current assets divided by total current liabilities.

Current assets include cash, accounts and notes receivable, inventory, and marketable securities. This ratio measures the degree to which current assets cover current liabilities. The higher the ratio the more assurance exists that you can retire the current liabilities. The current ratio measures the margin of safety available to cover any possible shrinkage in the value of current assets. Normally a ratio of 2:1 or higher is good.

Debt-to-equity ratio. Total liabilities divided by total net worth.

Sizable debt can burden a firm with substantial interest charges. Generally, total liabilities shouldn't exceed net worth, since the creditors have more at stake than the owners in such cases. You can analyze additional ratios by comparing current liabilities to net worth and fixed assets to net worth.

Efficiency Ratios

Receivables turnover. Total annual credit sales divided by average accounts receivable.

Receivables turnover analysis assists you in determining collection efficiency and quality of receivables. Compare your turnover with industry norms. Divide the turnover number into 365 days to determine the average number of days it takes to collect on receivables. Compare this with your credit terms. Generally, any collection period more than one-third over normal credit terms, such as forty days for thirty-day terms, is indicative of some slow-turning receivables. Reassess your credit policies and collection methods.

Inventory turnover. Total annual net sales divided by average inventory.

Inventory control is a prime management objective. Poor controls allow inventory to become costly to store, obsolete, or insufficient to meet demands. The sales-to-inventory relationship is a guide to the rapidity at which merchandise is being moved, and the effect on the flow of funds into the business. This ratio varies widely between different lines of business, and a company's figure is only meaningful when compared with industry norms. Carefully examine individual figures that are outside either the upper or lower quartiles for a given industry. Although low figures are usually the biggest problem, as they indicate excessively high inventories, extremely high turnovers might reflect insufficient merchandise to meet customer demand, and result in lost sales. Divide the turnover number into 365 days to determine the average number of days it takes to sell inventory. You generally want to turn inventory into sales (inventory turnover) and sales into cash (receivables turnover) as quickly as possible. Increase the number of operating cycles (cash to inventory to receivables to cash) in a year, and you increase your efficiency, liquidity, and eventual profitability.

Asset turnover. Total annual net sales divided by total assets.

Asset turnover ties in sales and the total investment that you use to generate those sales. While figures vary greatly from industry to industry, by comparing a company's turnover with industry norms, you can determine whether a firm is overtrading or undertrading. Overtrading means handling an excessive volume of sales in relation to investment. Undertrading means not generating sufficient sales to warrant the assets invested. An extremely low turnover (below the lower quartile) can be the result of excessively conservative or poor sales management. This indicates you need to follow a more aggressive sales policy. An extremely high turnover (above the upper quartile) could indicate overtrading, which may lead to financial difficulties.

Profitability Ratios

Return on sales. Net profit after taxes divided by total annual net sales.

This reveals the profits earned per dollar of sales. Return must be adequate for the firm to achieve satisfactory profits for its owners. This ratio is an indicator of the firm's ability to withstand adverse conditions such as falling prices, rising costs, and declining sales.

Return on assets. Net profit after taxes divided by total assets.

This ratio is the key indicator of profitability for a firm. It matches operating profits with the assets available to earn a return. Companies efficiently using their assets will have a high return, while less well-run businesses will have a low return.

Return on equity. Net profit after taxes divided by total net worth.

Use this ratio to analyze the ability of the firm's management to realize an adequate return on the capital invested by the owners. The tendency is to look increasingly to this ratio as a final criterion of profitability. Generally, a relationship of at least 10 percent is a desirable objective.

Cash and Tax Management

Cash is king in every business, but especially in small business. You cannot run out of cash, and you don't even want to run low. Good cash management techniques involve maximizing the amount and minimizing the time to *receive* money, as well as minimizing the amount and maximizing the time to *pay* out money. Here are a few tips to consider in your business:

Controlling Cash Receipts

- Require full payment or at least partial payment up front.

- Give a financial incentive for paying up front.
- Accept credit cards that allow you to get an immediate cash credit in your merchant account.
- Verify credit-worthiness before selling on credit.
- Charge interest and late payment penalties.
- Bill all sales promptly.
- Develop a strong and consistent collection policy.
- Factor (sell at a discount) account receivables.
- Sell nonproducing assets and old inventory.
- Deposit all cash and checks promptly.
- Avoid bank charges.
- Maintain an interest-bearing account.

Controlling Cash Disbursements

- Lease rather than buy.
- If able to pay all in cash, ask for a discount.
- Don't pay bills far in advance of due date unless there is a discount.
- Pay on the installment basis.
- Use credit cards for purchases.
- Delay the frequency of payroll and reimbursements.
- Pay sales commissions only after you collect receivables.
- Minimize investment in inventory.
- Purchase in volume for quantity discounts.
- Avoid unnecessary purchases.
- Use barter whenever possible.
- Arrange advertising to take advantage of media rate reductions.
- Consider buying used equipment.
- Purchase from discount stores.
- Obtain at least three bids for major product or service purchases.
- Ask for discounts: cash, trade, seasonal, quantity.
- Don't be afraid to negotiate price and terms.
- Research ways to reduce postage and telephone costs.
- Reward employees for cost reduction tips.
- Maintain security over customer and employee theft.

- Consider noncash and nonincome forms of employee compensation.
- Link compensation to performance.
- Eliminate unnecessary utility costs.
- Sublet unused office space.
- Closely monitor entertainment and travel expenses.
- Research ways to reduce insurance premiums.
- Use independent contractors or leased employees if possible.
- Use part-time employees.
- Eliminate overtime compensation.
- Eliminate unproductive meetings.
- Expand business hours since you're paying for the space anyway.

Good records with solid backup of all amounts claimed are very important for accurate tax preparation. Specific tax rules and regulations change constantly, so this discussion does not focus on the details of current tax law. However, some concepts will likely never change when it comes to your business and the tax law.

Here are a few tips to assist in your business tax planning:

- Maintain a separate business checking account, and keep all personal expenses out of it.
- Use credit cards for simpler and more accurate recordkeeping.
- Avoid paying cash for business items. If you must, obtain a receipt.
- Keep a regular mileage log for business automobile data.
- Document and take the deduction for office-in-the-home if you qualify.
- Check the current coverage and deduction rules for fringe benefit plans.
- Take advantage of IRAs, SEP-IRAs, and pension and profit-sharing plans.
- Maintain detailed records to justify and verify business travel, entertainment, and education expenses.
- Consider using per-diem rates for away-from-home travel.

- Consider hiring your children or spouse in the business to shift income, reduce taxes, and cover them with fringe benefits or pension plans.
- Utilize the equipment expensing rules to obtain an immediate tax deduction for depreciable items.
- Claim all ordinary, necessary, and reasonable business expenses you can verify and justify.
- If losing money in the early years, take advantage of the Net Operating Loss rules.
- Use an experienced, creative, ethical CPA or tax accountant to prepare your return and provide tax planning advice.

Call the IRS at (800) 829-3676 to request the following publications and forms (IRS charges a small fee for some):

Pub:	Title:
1	Your Rights as a Taxpayer
15	Circular E—Employer's Tax Guide
17	Your Federal Income Tax (for individuals)
334	Tax Guide for Small Business
463	Travel, Entertainment, and Gift Expenses
535	Business Expenses
560	Retirement Plans for the Self-Employed
583	Starting a Business and Keeping Records
587	Business Use of Your Home
910	Guide to Free Tax Services
917	Business Use of a Car

Form:	Title:
SS-4	Application for Employer Identification Number
SS-8	Determination of Employee Work Status (versus independent contractor)
W-4	Employer's Withholding Allowance Certificate
W-9	Request for Taxpayer ID Number and Certification

CHAPTER 18
ACTION ITEMS

Accounting and Financial Management

1. Develop a chart of accounts for your business.

2. Complete a break-even analysis for your business using best-case, worst-case, and most-likely-case scenarios.

3. Review RMA or D&B for key business ratios of your industry.

CHAPTER 19

Risk Management and Insurance

Winning a $10 million state lottery after paying $1 to enter is something we can all dream of, but will not likely experience. The lottery and other forms of gambling are examples of *speculative risk*. You have the chance to gain or lose. If your number is not picked, you lose your investment. If your number *is* picked, you win a prize. Investments in stocks and real estate are also examples of speculative risk. You can either make or lose money.

In business, there are many examples of speculative risk. Just going into business is a speculative risk. If it becomes successful, you gain. If it loses money or goes bankrupt, you lose. Deciding whether to introduce a new product or enter a new market is a speculative risk. Deciding whether or where to advertise is a speculative risk. You make decisions on speculative risk throughout your business life. Carefully weigh the costs and benefits, try to minimize the downside, and then make an informed decision on what action to take.

Pure risk, on the other hand, is risk that cannot produce a gain. It will either result in a loss or no loss (break-even). Examples include fire, death of a key person, bankruptcy of a customer, and theft. Pure risks are those that relate specifically to your business. Often, there is little you can do to completely eliminate pure risks, but there are several ways to handle them. The important first step is to properly identify such risks. Next, make a reasoned decision on how to handle them. This chapter concentrates on identifying and intelligently handling pure risks.

A third type of risk is *fundamental risk*. It differs from both pure risk and speculative risk in its impersonality. It plays no favorites. It does not single out one venture and bypass all others. Fundamental risk usually arises from the economic, political, social, or natural forces acting on society. There is little you can do other than try to predict and react appropriately. However, you can handle some fundamental risks similarly to pure risks. Examples of fundamental risks that affect many businesses include inflation, war, shortages, boycotts, technology, and drought.

Start your business risk analysis early in the planning stage. You may discover some major concerns that dramatically affect your other business decisions and choices. You don't want surprises later.

RISK IDENTIFICATION AND ANALYSIS

It's important for you, perhaps with the help of a good insurance agent, to develop an effective program of risk management. Pinpoint all the risks that may cause losses, estimate how severe those losses may be, and then select the best way to treat each risk.

Once you identify the risks, you generally have four possible ways to deal with them. In some cases, you may use a combination of methods. You can

1. Avoid the risk entirely.
2. Assume or absorb the risk yourself.
3. Prevent the occurrence or reduce the chances of occurrence or severity of the risk.
4. Transfer or shift the risk of loss to others by contract.

You can avoid risk in many ways. Leasing equipment, instead of buying it, bypasses the ownership risks. Incorporating your business avoids some personal liability risks. Keeping no more than $200 in the cash register at any time avoids the risk of losing more than $200 from theft. Leasing employees, or using temporary employment agencies, avoids the risk of dealing with employment law and tax issues.

Many risks you assume and absorb yourself, either because insurance or other methods of risk transfer are not available, or they are too expensive. An example of risk assumption is the deductible portion of any insurance policy. If a risk is measurable, you may want to set aside cash or reserves for self-insurance purposes.

You can prevent the occurrence of a loss, reduce the chance for a loss, or reduce the severity of a loss in many areas of the business. Here are a few examples of common business risks and ways to prevent or reduce them:

Protecting Against Shoplifters and Theft

- Hire security guards.
- Have good alarms and locks.
- Post antishoplifting signs warning of prosecution.
- Install convex mirrors, one-way mirrors, and cameras for monitoring.
- Use electronic signaling devices on expensive items.
- Place easily stolen small items near the cash register.
- Use hard-to-break plastic strings on clothing.
- Maintain sufficient personnel to cover floor space.
- Prosecute all shoplifters, even first offenders.
- Train employees to be visible, attentive, and aware.
- Install alarms on emergency exits.
- Display expensive items in security cases.
- Reduce clutter and arrange merchandise so that you can easily detect any unexplained gaps on shelves.
- Channel the flow of customers past the cashier, and block off unused checkout stands.
- Monitor fitting rooms.
- Use bright lighting and large windows in checkout areas.
- Keep minimum amounts of cash in the register.
- Ask the police to do a *walk-through* of your store, and point out vulnerabilities.

Protecting Against Employee Theft

- Screen job applicants carefully, and check references and police records.

- Use appropriate testing for prospective employees.
- Monitor employee-only areas.
- Monitor trash handling and employee packages.
- Use fidelity bonds (insurance covering theft) on employees.
- Limit access to warehouse and storage areas.
- Develop solid inventory and internal control procedures.
- Have a step-by-step cash-handling procedure with protections in place.
- Separate money-handling and money-recording procedures.
- Use sequentially numbered checks, price tickets, sales slips, and requisitions.
- Avoid employee parking near your receiving door.
- Change locks regularly if you have frequent employee turnover.
- Monitor returns and refunds carefully.
- Immediately terminate employees caught stealing, and report them to law enforcement.
- Rotate security guards to prevent monotony and fraternizing with other employees.
- Price retail items by machine or rubber stamp, not by handwriting.
- Restrict price setting and marking to authorized employees.
- Limit access to the loading dock.

Preventing Injuries to Workers

- Design the shops and offices to minimize chance of injury.
- Hold safety education programs for workers.
- Inspect and repair safety devices regularly.
- Allow only trained personnel to operate hazardous machinery.
- Use approved containers for flammable or hazardous materials.
- Keep all exits clear.
- Keep the workplace clean.

- Check for proper ventilation.
- Provide protective goggles and other protective equipment.
- Keep first aid supplies on hand.
- Post emergency telephone numbers.
- Instruct everyone on emergency procedures.

Preventing Losses Due to Fire

- Install an automatic sprinkler system.
- Purchase and maintain sufficient portable fire extinguishers.
- Install a fire alarm system or individual fire alarms.
- Install smoke detectors.
- Instruct all employees in the proper use of fire extinguishers.
- Post no-smoking signs in unsafe areas.
- Routinely check all electrical outlets, wires, and plugs.
- Ask the fire department to do a *walk-through* of your business and point out vulnerabilities.

Preventing Product Liability Claims

- Develop a quality control program to prevent defective merchandise from being sold.
- Provide adequate instructions for using all products.
- Post disclaimers, or have customers sign disclaimers when appropriate.
- Post any necessary warnings.

The most common way to transfer risk to others through contract is with insurance. The remainder of this chapter covers insurance issues. However, there are additional ways to transfer risk through contracts. Consider using provisions to transfer or limit your risk of loss when contracting to buy and sell, or to perform services. Use indemnification clauses in contracts such as leases if appropriate. Using options and hedging price changes are other ways some businesses transfer the risk of loss.

Liability and Property Insurance

You usually purchase business liability and property insurance for one of three reasons:

1. You make your own decision to transfer the risk of loss to an insurance company in exchange for a premium payment.
2. Your lender requires you to purchase certain insurance coverage.
3. Your landlord requires you to purchase certain insurance coverage.

First, consider liability insurance coverage because of potential large judgments, especially if there is the possibility of personal injury or death. Liability insurance covers your liability to third parties for personal injury damage or damage to property.

Address your liability coverage needs in this order:

- Workers' compensation
- General Liability
- Vehicle liability
- Products liability
- Professional liability

Workers' compensation insurance covers your liability for injuries received by employees on the job. It is mandatory and covers such injuries whether or not the business was negligent. Rates vary depending on the industry and occupation. There are no awards for pain and suffering or mental anguish. However, increasing numbers of injury claims are for job-related mental or emotional stress. The four benefits that workers' compensation covers are medical care, temporary disability at two-thirds of lost wages, lump-sum payments for permanent disability, and vocational rehabilitation. Compare private insurance premiums with the state compensation fund rates.

You only need workers' compensation for employees, not for independent contractors. Make sure you have properly classified workers, however, as discussed in chapter 17, so there can be no surprising claims for coverage. If you hire an independent contractor who has employees, insist on seeing a certificate of insurance establishing that the contractor is covering the employees for workers' compensation.

Your business can be legally liable to people injured and for property damaged, because you or your employees didn't use reasonable care. Judges and juries are increasingly generous in awarding damages, and an injured person can collect, not only for lost wages and medical bills, but also for intangibles like pain, suffering, and mental anguish. You need general liability insurance to protect you.

General liability policies protect you against judgments up to the amount of the policy limit plus the cost of defending the suit. They provide coverage for many common perils, including slip and fall, libel, slander, and false arrest, with a dollar limit per occurrence and an aggregate dollar limit for the year. They often exclude punitive damages and damages that result from intentional acts. Liability for defective products and for vehicles often requires additional insurance discussed below.

You need **vehicle liability** insurance to cover liability for the business's own cars and trucks, as well as employees' cars and trucks when used for business purposes. Check your employees' driving records before entrusting company vehicles to them, or sending them on business errands using their own cars. Ensure that you have coverage on any leased vehicles.

Products liability insurance covers liability for injuries caused by products you design, manufacture, or sell. You may be liable to a person injured by a defective product, or one that came without adequate instructions or warnings. Carefully analyze your needs for such insurance. Check the coverage and rates available. If possible and feasible, protect yourself with indemnification, hold harmless, and disclaimer provisions in your contracts.

Also consider **professional liability** insurance, sometimes termed malpractice or *errors and omissions* insurance. Coverage is available for doctors, lawyers, accountants, financial planners, engineers, architects, and many others. Determine whether such coverage is available for your business. Analyze the coverage, exclusions, and cost. Check with your professional and trade associations. They often sponsor cost-effective programs.

Business property insurance requires you to answer four questions:

1. What property should you insure?
2. What risks and perils will you cover?

3. What amount of insurance should you carry?
4. Should you buy replacement cost or present value coverage?

Read the policy closely to determine the exact property coverage. If you own the building, be sure to cover the building plus completed additions, permanent fixtures, outdoor fixtures, additions under construction, and temporary structures. Make sure business personal property coverage includes furniture and fixtures, machinery and equipment, inventory, raw materials, books, and tapes. Also cover any leased property that is your legal responsibility. Consider the need to cover customer property of which you have custody, and any property in transit. Note the typical exclusions of accounting records, currency, jewelry, securities, signs, and vehicles. Obtain separate coverage or add a rider covering any additional needs.

Most business property insurance is either Basic Form, Broad Form, or Special Form.

Basic Form coverage includes losses caused by these risks:

- Fire
- Lightning
- Explosion
- Windstorm or hail
- Smoke
- Aircraft or vehicles
- Riot
- Vandalism
- Sprinkler leaks
- Sinkholes
- Volcanoes

The policy defines these perils. It also lists some exclusions, such as nuclear hazards, power failures, or mud slides.

Broad Form coverage contains everything that's in the Basic Form, and adds protection from a few more perils, including glass breakage, falling objects, weight of snow or ice, and water damage. It specifically defines coverage and lists some exclusions.

Special Form policies offer wider and slightly more expensive coverage. They cover *all risks* of physical loss unless the policy specifically excludes or limits the loss. This type of policy offers the most protection. Seriously consider it. It covers loss by theft, which the Basic and Broad Form policies don't cover. If you need specific coverage that the forms don't include, such as flood or earthquake coverage, you can often add it by paying an additional premium.

Carry enough insurance on your building to rebuild it, but don't overinsure the value. You need coverage only for the building, not the land, and you will not be able to recover more than the actual damage. If you're unsure of the value, obtain an appraisal. Be careful not to underinsure. Even though most losses are not total losses, co-insurance clauses often require you to insure at least 80 percent of the property's replacement cost or actual cash value. If you don't, you become a co-insurer of the property.

Historically, property insurance covered the actual cash value of the property, which in many cases was not sufficient to replace the property. Today, if available, you generally want a replacement cost policy that will put you back in the position you were in before the loss. It will pay enough to cover the cost of new buildings and other property. An actual cash value policy will pay only replacement cost less physical depreciation of the destroyed or damaged property.

If you are a tenant, read your lease carefully to determine what your liabilities are and what insurance coverage the lease requires. Leases often require liability insurance coverage of at least $1 million. Check coverage and rates for renters' commercial policies to cover other risks.

Besides the general liability and property coverage discussed above, there may be other related insurance coverage you need. Consider fidelity bonds to cover employees handling money. Look into crime insurance coverage to add or increase defined crimes or specific property covered, including property in transit. Maintain good records to document loss and value. Consider business interruption insurance that will cover your lost profits. It will also pay your overhead business expenses while your business is temporarily closed after some casualty. Decide if your specific industry has special insurance needs, such as liquor liability.

You can't afford to optimally insure your business against every possible risk. First, cover those areas required by law or contract. Next, prioritize insurance to cover the types of losses that could destroy the business or seriously threaten its continuation. Be less concerned about smaller losses.

The following tips can help you save money on your insurance:

- Increase the amount of your deductibles.
- Initiate loss-prevention and risk-reduction measures.
- Comparison shop for rates and coverage.
- Contractually transfer risk to others.

- Find comprehensive insurance packages when available.
- Seek out group plans.
- Consider using an *umbrella* policy to provide liability insurance beyond the basic policy and to cover any potential gaps.

HEALTH, DISABILITY, AND LIFE INSURANCE

After you have adequately insured all your property and liability risks, consider using group insurance as a fringe benefit for you and your employees. Group plans for health, disability, and life insurance coverage are common and popular.

Group insurance offers these benefits to your employees:

- It establishes a solid insurance foundation that employees would not voluntarily acquire.
- The employee has protection in the case of illness, death, or disability.
- The premiums are generally not taxable to the employee.
- Group plans generally cost less than individual policies.
- There is greater after-tax value to the employee than a wage increase.
- Conversion or portability provisions may be available.

Group insurance offers these benefits to your business:

- The contribution is generally tax-deductible.
- It helps the employer attract and retain quality people.
- It enhances employee morale and productivity.
- It promotes good public relations and good employee relations.

Group medical plans are generally comprehensive major medical plans. These plans provide broad coverage and protection against large, unpredictable medical expenses. They cover a wide range of medical care charges with few limits and usually high lifetime benefits. Vision coverage is sometimes a separate coverage. Check your plan carefully.

Group medical plans often require the insured to meet a certain deductible level, and then the plan pays a specified percentage (usually 80 percent) of covered hospital, surgical, and medical expenses. Once the insured pays a certain amount of out-of-pocket expense, the plan pays 100 percent of eligible charges for the remainder of the calendar year, up to the lifetime maximum limit.

Many major medical plans include cost containment provisions intended to help manage escalating medical costs. Typically, these plans require that hospital stays and surgeries be reviewed by the insurer before the patient receives treatment. In addition, the plans usually offer financial incentives if a client obtains cost-effective medical treatment.

A number of insurance companies offer Preferred Provider Organization (PPO) plans. PPO plans encourage insiders to use an established network of "preferred" providers whom the insurer has contracted with to provide services. When you use the preferred providers, the plan pays a larger percentage of the medical bill. If a client chooses to use a nonpreferred provider, the client usually pays more in out-of-pocket expense.

Health Maintenance Organization (HMO) plans also provide comprehensive health care. Members pay fixed monthly fees. In return, they receive health care service as often as they need it. An HMO usually requires that medical services be reviewed and approved by participating providers to be covered under the plan.

Group dental plans provide reimbursement for dental services, including preventive care. Dental plans normally classify expenses into the following categories:

- Preventive (oral exams and cleaning)
- Basic (fillings and extractions)
- Major (crowns, partials, and full dentures)
- Orthodontia (teeth straightening)

Dental plans normally have deductibles ranging from $25 to $100. The deductible applies to each individual during each calendar year. To encourage preventive care, many plans do not apply the deductible to preventive-care expenses. The insured pays some percentage of the dentist charge in most plans.

Group disability insurance provides reimbursement for the loss of income resulting from disability caused by sickness or accident.

Short-term disability income insurance replaces a portion of lost income for a limited period of time, usually for periods up to either thirteen, twenty-six, or fifty-two weeks. Long-term disability income pays benefits for periods substantially greater than one year, often until age sixty-five or to the employee's retirement age.

Group life insurance is usually yearly renewable term life insurance. There is no cash value accumulation, and premium rates increase yearly, or in five- to ten-year intervals, based on the employee's attained age. Group life insurance often automatically includes group accidental death and dismemberment. It pays an additional benefit if death is the result of an accident. Optional dependent life that provides life insurance coverage for a dependent spouse and children may also be available.

Voluntary term life insurance supplements basic term life insurance. It gives employees flexibility in selecting the amount of coverage that meets their needs. The employee typically pays for this coverage.

Life and disability insurance may also be appropriate for a business to protect its own financial loss through the death or disability of a key employee or owner. They can also help fund future buyouts of owners after death or disability.

CHAPTER 19
ACTION ITEMS

Risk Management and Insurance

1. Identify the largest risks in your business, and determine how best to handle them.

2. Prioritize your top three insurance needs.

3. Select one risk and list all possible ways to prevent or minimize losses.

CHAPTER 20

Twelve Tips for Business Success

It is not easy to start and insure the success of business today. Statistics show that only one out of five businesses started today will still be in business five years from now. However, if you learn and apply the twelve tips that follow, you will greatly enhance your chances for success. Some of these tips review concepts previously discussed. Others are new thoughts. Keep them all in mind as you start your business. Review them periodically to make sure you remain on track.

How do self-made millionaires make their money? Research shows that, of today's self-made millionaires, approximately 10 percent made it as highly paid executives in the corporate world, 10 percent made it as professionals (doctors, lawyers, and so forth), 5 percent made it in sales, and 1 percent made it in miscellaneous activities such as entertainment, inventions, lottery, and so on. However, a full 74 percent of self-made millionaires made their money with their own businesses (including real estate as a business). Entrepreneurs control and optimize their chance to make a fortune.

TIP #1: DO WHAT YOU LOVE.

You will spend many hours and many weekends working in and on your new business. If you commit all that time to a business, make sure that it's something you truly enjoy. If you do something you love, it shows, and the money follows. If you do something only for the money, it also shows, and you never realize your full potential.

Most people need to work to make a living, and it's unreasonable to expect anyone to work without considering the potential profit. Here's a helpful exercise to determine whether this planned business is your correct choice: Imagine that you have inherited a large sum of money and would never have to work another day in your life. Would you still want to go into this business? If you can truly answer yes, then this is the business for you.

Confucius said: "Choose a job you love, and you will never have to work a day in your life." Abraham Maslow eloquently proclaimed:

A musician must make music,
an artist must paint, a poet must write
if he is ultimately to be at peace with himself.
What one can be, one must be.

Tip #2: Have sufficient experience.

You dramatically increase your chances for success in starting a business if you have some experience. Ideally, you should have three to five years of experience in the industry you are entering. The more positions you have held, the more companies you have worked for, and the more practical experience you have been able to obtain on the job, the greater your chances for success.

If you start a business in which you have absolutely no experience, seriously reconsider your decision and options. Think about redirecting yourself toward an area where you have some experience. Alternatively, spend a few years working for someone else and learning about the new industry before venturing out on your own.

Should you choose to work for someone else, make sure that you give a 100 percent effort to that business. Recognize the great advantage that you have of being paid for on-the-job training. Analyze and learn from the decision-making and management strategies of your employer. Develop the mind-set of an entrepreneur while working for someone else.

Set a personal goal of becoming an expert in your field, the best in your business. Constantly strive to learn more and improve.

TIP #3: IMPROVE ON AN EXISTING PRODUCT OR SERVICE.

Some completely new products and completely new services are overnight successes. However, 98 percent of all new products and services do not succeed.

You greatly increase your chance for success if you improve on an already-existing, proven product or service. Of course, you need to add some value to differentiate your product or service, but this modification doesn't have to be extensive. A mere 10 percent to 20 percent improvement is dramatic. It can revolutionize an industry and dominate a market.

Find an aspect of a product that needs change or improvement, or bring the product to a new market. You don't have to reinvent the wheel. Do what you do better, and do it a little differently from everyone else. That may be enough.

Review the fourteen points for the transformation of management and the seven deadly diseases that management guru W. Edwards Deming described in *Out of Crisis*. Concentrating on them can dramatically improve company performance. In summary form, they are as follows:

Deming's Fourteen Points for the Transformation of Management

1. Create constancy of purpose for improvement of product and service. The company's role should be to stay in business and provide jobs through innovation, research, constant improvement, and maintenance.
2. Adopt the new philosophy. Mistakes and negativism are unacceptable.
3. Cease dependence on mass inspection. Improve the process so that there are no defects.
4. End the practice of awarding business on the price tag alone. Seek the best quality in a long-term relationship with a single supplier.
5. Improve constantly and forever the system of production and service. Continually look for ways to reduce waste and improve quality.

6. Institute training on the job.
7. Institute leadership. Help people do a better job and learn by objective methods.
8. Drive out fear. Assure better quality and productivity by making people feel secure.
9. Break down barriers between staff areas. Work as a team to solve and foresee problems.
10. Eliminate slogans, exhortations, and targets for the work force. Let workers formulate their own slogans.
11. Eliminate numerical quotas. Concentrate on quality and methods rather than only numbers.
12. Remove barriers to pride of workmanship. Allow people to do a good job and enjoy it.
13. Institute a vigorous program of education and retraining. Include teamwork and statistical techniques.
14. Take action to accomplish the transformation. Everyone must understand the plan of action to carry out the quality mission.

Deming's Seven Deadly Diseases

1. Lack of constancy of purpose. If the company has no long-range plans, management and the employees are insecure.
2. Emphasis on short-term profits. This can undermine quality and productivity.
3. Evaluation by performance, merit rating, or annual review of performance. This destroys teamwork and nurtures rivalry. Performance ratings build fear and leave people bitter, despondent, and beaten. They encourage defection.
4. Mobility of management. Job-hopping managers never understand the companies they work for and are never there long enough to follow through on long-term changes that are necessary for quality and productivity.
5. Running a company on visible figures alone. The most important figures, such as happy customers, are often unknown.
6. Excessive medical costs for employee health care. These increase the final costs of goods and services.
7. Excessive warranty and product liability costs fueled by attorney contingent fees.

TIP #4: CONCENTRATE ON A NARROW AND DEEP TARGET MARKET.

Your target market is the ideal customer to whom you market your product or service. The more narrowly you define the target market, the better you can satisfy your customer.

You can use a variety of methods to define your target market. The more of these that you can use accurately, the better. Use geographics to define your customer by locations such as city, state, and country. Use demographics to define your customer by characteristics such as sex, age, education, religion, and marital status. Use psychographics, the most difficult classification, to classify your customer by lifestyle and habits. Market research and market testing, as well as customer analysis and common sense, can all be used to help narrowly define your target market.

Your target market needs to be deep as well as narrow. A deep target market is a market that has sufficient customers you can economically reach to justify the business. You don't want a very narrow market that has too few people to justify producing products and services. You also don't want a target market that may be large in numbers, but too dispersed geographically to be reached efficiently.

Research your market. Use common sense and solid judgment to narrow the market sufficiently. Many more businesses have made the mistake of not defining their markets narrowly enough than have targeted a market that is too narrow or shallow.

TIP #5: DEVELOP A UNIQUE SELLING PROPOSITION (USP).

A USP is crucial to the identity and success of any business. However, it is amazing that many businesses don't have one. A USP is that distinct and appealing idea that sets your business apart from every other "me too" competitor. Build your entire marketing and operational success upon your USP. It is the distinguishing advantage you will hold out in all your marketing, advertising, and sales efforts. It is the philosophical foundation of your business. Its essence should pervade everything you do.

Think about your business! Why should a customer use your products or services rather than those of a competitor? If you have no answer, then your business may be "just getting by." You're not fully utilizing your resources, and you won't reach your full potential.

The USP for Domino's Pizza is "hot, fresh pizza at your door in thirty minutes or you get it free." Federal Express's USP is "when you absolutely, positively have to have it overnight." These are two clear examples of solid, memorable USPs that have been prime ingredients for the success enjoyed by both companies.

Identify the needs in your industry that are going unfulfilled. Capitalize on one, two, or three of those unfulfilled needs, and build it into your USP. Make sure all your employees know it as well as you.

Be specific in defining your USP. *Quality, service,* and *low price* sound fine, but you must be more specific to make the claims believable.

Tip #6: Have a written business plan.

If you try to obtain outside financing from a bank or investors, they will require a written business plan. However, even if you use your own money to start and grow the new business, prepare a written business plan for your own use.

There are many books on the subject, and there are several computer software packages that can assist you in developing a business plan. The important point is not the format you use, but that you make the decisions on paper before making them in the business. With a written business plan, you might discover an issue you didn't consider, or a potential stumbling block. You still have time to obtain additional information, alter your course, plan for the inevitable, or perhaps even terminate the business temporarily or permanently.

Your business plan is a road map for your business. It will not turn out as you planned, and you will be making constant changes, but at least you'll be in control.

The actual format and order of the plan are not critically important. However, be sure to cover the three primary activities of operations, finance, and marketing. If the plan is being viewed by outside parties, prepare a brief executive summary, highlighting the essence of your business.

Tip #7: Prepare a two-year cash flow statement.

Your business plan should project both profitability and liquidity. Your income statement shows profitability. Your cash flow statement shows liquidity. Many new businesses that start with a good idea never reach their potential because they run out of cash and are unable to continue.

Prepare a two-year cash flow projection under a worst-case scenario. Ensure that you have sufficient cash resources on hand, or the capability of accessing them, to survive for the two-year period and continue operations at the same time.

When determining cash needs, consider the costs of business research and analysis, start-up (all items necessary before opening the doors), and operations. Also, make sure you have sufficient cash resources for personal living expenses.

You hope the worst case does not develop, but it is good to plan for that outcome. If you are still liquid and able to continue under this scenario, you have improved your chances for success, and you are in a good cash position to start the business.

Tip #8: Develop a marketing mind-set.

As you run your business, develop a *marketing orientation* rather than a *production orientation*. With a marketing orientation or marketing mind-set, you view everything through the customer's eyes. You make decisions based on what is better for the customer, not necessarily what is better for you or what will make your job or your employees' jobs easier.

An easy business rule to remember is that "if you keep your customers happy, you keep your customers." A well-publicized study that surveyed customers and analyzed why they stopped doing business with companies made the following findings:

- 1%   Died or became incapacitated
- 3%   Moved away
- 5%   Were influenced by friends
- 9%   Were lured away by the competition
- 14%   Became dissatisfied with the product or service
- 68%   Were turned away by an employee's attitude of indifference

Make sure you care about the customer, and that the customer knows it. *Perception* of value and service is what is important to the customer.

Develop a vibrant USP, and stress to the customer the *benefits*, instead of the features, of your product or service. Continually add value to your product or services. Constantly test prices, sales techniques, colors, premiums, locations, hours, and so forth. Always look for a better, more efficient way to do business and to give your customers better service.

Use strong guarantees for customer satisfaction in your products and services. Be more concerned with marketing as a whole than with just advertising. Add value and *test, test, test!*

The L. L. Bean Company, famed for mail-order success, excellent merchandise, and superb service, ingrains in its employees the following philosophy:

- Customers are the most important people ever in this office, in person, or by mail.
- Customers are not dependent on us. We are dependent on them.
- Customers are not an interruption of our work. They are the purpose of it. We are not doing them a favor by serving them. They are doing us a favor by giving us the opportunity to do so.
- Customers are not people with whom to argue or match wits. Nobody ever won an argument with a customer.
- Customers are people who bring us their wants. It is our job to handle them profitably to them and to ourselves.

TIP #9: TREAT YOUR BUSINESS AS A FRANCHISE.

It is not by accident that most people who buy a franchise end up with a successful business, and that most people who start their own businesses do not succeed. Franchisors test and improve the best franchises through years of experience and mistakes, so you won't make those same mistakes.

Treat your business as if it were a franchise. Work *on* the business, not *in* the business. Work to produce a turnkey operation, developed over the years by a series of tests, successes and failures, and a good set of systems.

The successful turnkey business that you develop should almost run itself. Its success does not require the owner's actual presence. Visualize your business as you want it to be in the future. Do everything necessary to get to that point.

Chances are that you will never franchise your business. However, running it with the thought that it is a franchise dramatically increases the chance for your business's success and continued growth. Learn to systematize, organize, and delegate well.

Tip #10: Grow to survive.

Living organisms start dying the minute they stop growing. Your business must grow to survive. This does not mean that you must increase sales, customers, or profit. Although those are goals for most businesses, growth can also be an increase in productivity or an increase in quality. However, the key is that you continue to improve in some way.

Leo Buscaglia emphasizes in his writings that, as a child, his parents encouraged him to learn something new each day and to share it with the family at their nightly dinner. Tony Robbins stresses the concept of CANI, which stands for "constant and never ending improvement." The Japanese business concept of *kaizen* stresses constant striving for improvement in small increments. Whether in your personal or business life, you must continually grow and improve. Don't stay in one place.

Go for changes that work and can lead to breathtaking improvements in performance. In *Reengineering the Corporation*, authors Michael Hammer and James Champy carefully define *reengineering* as "the *fundamental* rethinking and *radical* redesign of business *processes* to achieve *dramatic* improvements in critical, contemporary measures of performance, such as cost, quality, service, and speed." Take nothing for granted. Concentrate on what should be, not what is. Determine first what you must do, then how to do it. Constantly ask yourself, Why?

Tip #11: Form an advisory committee.

As smart as you are, you need help, feedback, and ideas. Entrepreneurship is often a lonely business. Become involved with a group of similar businesspeople who meet regularly to share ideas.

Form an advisory committee to meet periodically to advise you on business decisions.

An advisory committee is similar to a board of directors, but it meets and acts on a much more informal basis. It is subject to less legal liability than a board of directors. You can form your advisory committees on a fee-paid basis or on a reciprocal-service basis. Meet periodically to brainstorm, share ideas, and help solve problems. Important contacts, business, and referrals can also result.

Tip #12: Spend thirty minutes per day in quiet time.

It's easy to become bogged down in the details of running a business, and not find or take time to step back and visualize the big picture.

As Stephen Covey points out in *Seven Habits of Highly Successful People,* it is essential to concentrate on the things in your life that are *important,* but not necessarily *urgent.*

Reserve at least thirty minutes per day of quiet time where you have no distractions. Sit back, relax, close your eyes, and, with no particular agenda, just let the ideas and thoughts flow. Do this every day, if possible. You'll soon look forward to it. The brilliant insights and great new business ideas and solutions you develop will amaze you.

Spend a few minutes at the end of the day to praise yourself for all you have accomplished. Take a few minutes to forgive yourself for all your mistakes. Make a list of the things you need to tackle tomorrow. Thank someone every day. Thank your customers, employees, vendors, and your family.

Conclusion

Be honest with yourself. Be empathetic and open with others. Build and maintain self-confidence. Value and respect yourself. Make your own choices and decisions. Be excited about change. Be optimistic, enthusiastic, and hopeful. Visualize your success and utilize your creativity. Set and accomplish worthwhile and challenging goals. Love and respect others. Be friendly and supportive of family and friends.

Don't be defeated by temporary setbacks and failures. Remember that patience and persistence are the marks of a champion. Thomas Edison tried 10,000 combinations of ideas and materials before he found the combination that made the first successful light bulb. Babe Ruth struck out more times than any player in his era, but no one remembers or really cares about that statistic.

Consider this sorry record of a persistent person who eventually triumphed:

1831	Failed in business
1832	Defeated for legislature
1833	Failed in business
1834	Elected to legislature
1836	Suffered nervous breakdown
1838	Defeated for speaker
1840	Defeated for elector
1846	Elected to Congress
1855	Defeated for Senate
1856	Defeated for vice president
1858	Defeated for Senate
1860	Elected president

This person who suffered repeated failure was . . . Abraham Lincoln.

Many a successful person has achieved success at precisely the moment that they were sure that failure was certain . . . because they persisted. If you know this is the business for you, and you've discovered an unmet need or want, apply the concepts in this book. It is only a matter of time until you succeed. Be patient and persistent. Put the ideas expressed in this book and the twelve tips listed in this chapter into practice.

Best of luck to you in your business ventures. May you have lots of fun and make lots of money as a well-deserved byproduct.

INDEX

Information and Order Form

Fax orders: (619) 481-6519

Phone orders: Call (619) 481-1171. Have your credit card information ready.

On-line orders: tseveran@severance.com
Internet: http://www.severance.com

Mail orders: Tycoon Publishing
3809 Plaza Drive, #107-111
Oceanside, CA 92056
Phone: (619) 481-1171

Please send _____ additional copies of *Business Start-up Guide* at $19.95 per copy plus sales tax and shipping.

Please ❑ mail ❑ fax ❑ e-mail me your listing of additional books, tapes, reports, and seminars.

Name _____

Company Name _____

Address _____

City _____ State _____ Zip _____

Telephone ( ) _____ Fax ( ) _____

E-mail _____

Sales tax: Please add 7.75% for books shipped to California addresses.

Shipping: $4 for the first book and $2 for each additional book.
Payment: ❑ Check, payable to Tycoon Publishing
             ❑ Credit card
               ❑ Visa ❑ MasterCard ❑ AMEX ❑ Discover

Card Number _____

Name on Card _____ Exp. Date_____

Signature _____

Call and order now!

Information and Order Form

Fax orders: (619) 481-6519

Phone orders: Call (619) 481-1171. Have your credit card information ready.

On-line orders: tseveran@severance.com
Internet: http://www.severance.com

Mail orders: Tycoon Publishing
3809 Plaza Drive, #107-111
Oceanside, CA 92056
Phone: (619) 481-1171

Please send _____ additional copies of *Business Start-up Guide* at $19.95 per copy plus sales tax and shipping.

Please ❏ mail ❏ fax ❏ e-mail me your listing of additional books, tapes, reports, and seminars.

Name _____

Company Name _____

Address _____

City _____ State _____ Zip _____

Telephone ( ) _____ Fax ( ) _____

E-mail _____

Sales tax: Please add 7.75% for books shipped to California addresses.

Shipping: $4 for the first book and $2 for each additional book.

Payment: ❏ Check, payable to Tycoon Publishing
❏ Credit card
❏ Visa ❏ MasterCard ❏ AMEX ❏ Discover

Card Number _____

Name on Card _____ Exp. Date_____

Signature _____

Call and order now!

Information and Order Form

Fax orders: (619) 481-6519

Phone orders: Call (619) 481-1171. Have your credit card information ready.

On-line orders: tseveran@severance.com
Internet: http://www.severance.com

Mail orders: Tycoon Publishing
                     3809 Plaza Drive, #107-111
                     Oceanside, CA 92056
                     Phone: (619) 481-1171

Please send _____ additional copies of *Business Start-up Guide* at $19.95 per copy plus sales tax and shipping.

Please ☐ mail   ☐ fax   ☐ e-mail   me your listing of additional books, tapes, reports, and seminars.

Name _____

Company Name _____

Address _____

City _____ State _____ Zip _____

Telephone ( ) _____ Fax ( ) _____

E-mail _____

Sales tax: Please add 7.75% for books shipped to California addresses.

Shipping: $4 for the first book and $2 for each additional book.

Payment: ☐ Check, payable to Tycoon Publishing
             ☐ Credit card
                     ☐ Visa ☐ MasterCard ☐ AMEX ☐ Discover

Card Number _____

Name on Card _____ Exp. Date_____

Signature _____

Call and order now!

Information and Order Form

Fax orders: (619) 481-6519

Phone orders: Call (619) 481-1171. Have your credit card information ready.

On-line orders: tseveran@severance.com
Internet: http://www.severance.com

Mail orders: Tycoon Publishing
3809 Plaza Drive, #107-111
Oceanside, CA 92056
Phone: (619) 481-1171

Please send _____ additional copies of *Business Start-up Guide* at $19.95 per copy plus sales tax and shipping.

Please ☐ mail   ☐ fax   ☐ e-mail   me your listing of additional books, tapes, reports, and seminars.

Name _____

Company Name _____

Address _____

City _____ State _____ Zip _____

Telephone ( ) _____ Fax ( ) _____

E-mail _____

Sales tax: Please add 7.75% for books shipped to California addresses.

Shipping: $4 for the first book and $2 for each additional book.
Payment: ☐ Check, payable to Tycoon Publishing
☐ Credit card
☐ Visa ☐ MasterCard ☐ AMEX ☐ Discover

Card Number _____

Name on Card _____ Exp. Date_____

Signature _____

Call and order now!

Information and Order Form

Fax orders: (619) 481-6519

Phone orders: Call (619) 481-1171. Have your credit card information ready.

On-line orders: tseveran@severance.com
Internet: http://www.severance.com

Mail orders: Tycoon Publishing
3809 Plaza Drive, #107-111
Oceanside, CA 92056
Phone: (619) 481-1171

Please send _____ additional copies of *Business Start-up Guide* at $19.95 per copy plus sales tax and shipping.

Please ❏ mail ❏ fax ❏ e-mail me your listing of additional books, tapes, reports, and seminars.

Name _____

Company Name _____

Address _____

City _____ State _____ Zip _____

Telephone (___) _____ Fax (___) _____

E-mail _____

Sales tax: Please add 7.75% for books shipped to California addresses.

Shipping: $4 for the first book and $2 for each additional book.

Payment: ❏ Check, payable to Tycoon Publishing
            ❏ Credit card
              ❏ Visa   ❏ MasterCard   ❏ AMEX   ❏ Discover

Card Number _____

Name on Card _____ Exp. Date _____

Signature _____

Call and order now!